Also by Andrew O'Hagan

FICTION

Our Fathers
Personality
Be Near Me
The Life and Opinions of Maf the Dog
The Illuminations

NONFICTION

The Missing
The Atlantic Ocean

The
Secret
Life

The
Secret
Life

THREE

TRUE

STORIES

OF THE

DIGITAL AGE

Andrew O'Hagan

FARRAR, STRAUS AND GIROUX   NEW YORK

Farrar, Straus and Giroux
18 West 18th Street, New York 10011

Printed in the United States of America
Originally published in 2017 by Faber and Faber Limited, Great Britain
Published in the United States by Farrar, Straus and Giroux
First American edition, 2017

Library of Congress Cataloging-in-Publication Data
Names: O'Hagan, Andrew, 1968– author.
Title: The secret life : three true stories of the digital age / Andrew O'Hagan.
Description: First American edition. | New York : Farrar, Straus and Giroux, 2017.
Identifiers: LCCN 2017001315 | ISBN 9780374277918 (hardcover) | ISBN
    9780374717094 (ebook)
Subjects: LCSH: Online identities. | Secrecy.
Classification: LCC HM851 .O395 | DDC 302.3—dc23
LC record available at https://lccn.loc.gov/2017001315

Designed by Abby Kagan

www.fsgbooks.com
www.twitter.com/fsgbooks • www.facebook.com/fsgbooks

10   9   8   7   6   5   4   3   2   1

for Jane Swan

There is another world, but it is in this one.
                                    —PAUL ÉLUARD

Contents

Preface

When you write novels, you take from the world what you must, and give back what you can, and you take it for granted that the imagination is sovereign. But what happens when you are writing a reported story? Isn't it dictated by matters of fact and therefore outside the imagination? My proposition in this book is that the separation won't hold, especially not in the world now. When I'm reporting I feel less like a news gatherer and more like an actuality seeker, someone for whom the techniques of fiction are never foreign and seldom inappropriate. The people I write about tend to inhabit a reality that they make for themselves or that in other ways consorts with fiction, and one is required to enter their ether and dance with their shades in order to find the story. When I was a young reader, I learned from the poets not to trust reality—"reality is a cliché from which we escape by metaphor," Wallace Stevens wrote—and the leading figures in this nonfiction book, each of whom is real or began real, depend for their existence and their power in the world on a high degree of artificiality.

It is the habit of the times to organize the ironies embedded in this state of affairs and call it culture. (Just look at reality TV.) And the creative writer, given what I've said about metaphor, may have a head start when it comes to investigating that culture—which is why we would do well, now and then, to open the notepad and turn on the recording device. Asked which of the arts was closest to writing, Norman Mailer once told me the answer was "acting." He talked about an essential loss of ego, a circumstance that most people wouldn't associate with him. But the principle will be familiar to writers of fiction and nonfiction who are always on the lookout for a second life, believing it must be a writer's business to invest freely in self-transcendence. I believe that is what F. Scott Fitzgerald meant when he said there can be no reliable biography of a writer, because a writer "is too many people if he's any good."

We were addicted to the ailments of the Web long before we understood how the technology would change our lives. In a sense it gave the tools of fiction-making to everybody equally, so long as they had access to a computer and a willingness to swim into the Internet's deep well of otherness. J. G. Ballard predicted that the writer would no longer have a role in society—he would soon become superfluous, like those characters in nineteenth-century Russian novels. "Given that external reality is a fiction," Ballard wrote, "he does not need to invent the fiction because it is already there." Every day on the Web you see his point being made; it is a marketplace of selfhood. With e-mail, everyone can communicate both instantly and invisibly, as either themselves or someone else. There are 67 million "invented" names on Facebook, many of them clearly living another life, less ordinary, or at any rate less checkable. Nobody knows who they really are. Encryption has made the average user a ghost—an alias, a simulacrum, a reflection. In this climate, only our buying power makes us real, and what self we have is open to offers of improvement— new eye color, better insurance, slimmer body—from marketing firms and mobile-phone companies before they hand our data to governments, who aim to make us visible again in the interests of national security.

In W. H. Auden's "The Age of Anxiety," we meet Quant, a man who sees his own reflection in the mirror of a New York bar, surrounded by a "facetious culture," by which he means a factitious one. It seemed to Auden an aspect of modern life that a man might see no correspondence between his social or economic position and his private mental life. Quant speaks to himself in the mirror. "My double, my dear image," he says. "Is it lively there" in "that land of glass?" "Does your self like mine / Taste of untruth?" I think of Auden's poem when I consider the two generations who have now spent their time looking at the glass of their computer screens. What have we been looking for? Is it lively there? And have we grown addicted to the taste of untruth? The Internet offers a secret life to everybody, but how it happens, and who controls it, stirred me to write these stories. On every bright acre of the Web, your personal data is harvested to furnish a neural network, a global mind, and your reward is to feel you contain multitudes.

In 1964, thirteen years before Apple sold its first home computer, Joseph Mitchell opened a profile in *The New Yorker* with the following sentence: "Joe Gould was an odd and penniless and unemployable little man who came to the city in 1916 and ducked and dodged and held on as hard as he could for over thirty-five years." Mitchell had written about Gould in the magazine twenty-two years before, but his new profile, "Joe Gould's Secret," summoned the cloud of uncertainty surrounding the man's great masterwork, "The Oral History of Our Time," which Gould claimed to have spent several decades working on. Joseph Mitchell reported that Gould had never really started the book and it was all just blank pages. Yet, more recently, the writer Jill Lepore unearthed material from "The Oral History," and she demonstrates that "Joe Gould's Secret" has fictional elements. "Two writers guard an archive," Lepore says. "One writes Fiction; the other writes Fact. To get past them, you have to figure out which is which. Mitchell said that Gould made things up. But Gould said that Mitchell did." What we know for sure is that Joseph Mitchell had a secret of his own: he had never written a word of the Joycean novel about New York that he said he would write. He lived for more than thirty years after his second Joe Gould piece came out, but never published another word. The conversation between a writer and his subjects is often, as Wordsworth said, too deep for tears, and it can involve finding sentences for realities and correspondences that are invisible to the naked eye. Such difficulties have always interested me. They inform my sense of life. Moreover, I find that literature, formerly the main arena of double lives, now takes second place to the Web, where nobody today can be simply one thing.

The stories in this book were written from the wild west of the Internet, before policing or a code of decency. We still don't have good manners or clear professional ethics, and the new ontological arrangements of the Internet are yet to become second nature. I set out to write stories that might swim in the ethical mire of all that, and here they are, together. There is nothing general about these stories: even in the wider context of the Net, my three case studies are individual, and in many ways they are archetypal of nothing but themselves. The WikiLeaks founder, Julian Assange, is not a typical figure of the Internet Age any more than Charles Foster Kane is a typical character from the Age of Newspapers. The purported bitcoin creator Craig Wright is a highly eccentric respondent, on the cusp of digital currency, to the financial crisis of 2008, and his inner trials interested me for their own sake. Ronald Pinn, a digital person I invented based on a young man who died thirty years ago, is between them, a man of the moment perhaps but also an element in experimental journalism, a person both true and not true, around whom the question of existence swirls like snow. Every man has his own Rosebud, and it was never my intention to suggest that these three cases represent the whole Internet, or, heaven save us, the modern man of today. They fascinated me personally. In looking at arguments of power, freedom, transparency, corporate power, economic control, illicit markets, and the manipulation of identity, I found myself entangled with these three individuals. They might each tell a story about the times we are living in, but none of them is universal, and they come from what my editor, Alexander Star, described to me as "the bleeding edge of the Internet."

I have spoken of the way the Web has made self-creators of us all, yet the people I write about in this book, whether they like it or not, are both masters of the Internet and victims of it. These were men in trouble, and I felt I was reporting not merely from a cultural front but from a psychological one. In one way or another, these figures or their representatives sought me out, looking for someone to tell their story, but none of the stories I was able to tell is one they would have wanted. In each case it turned out to be a story about how an online self and a real self might constantly be at war with each other. All told, I spent several years in the company of these men, and they revealed to me—amid the buzz and boom and sludge of the Internet—that human problems remain human problems, and the higher work of computers doesn't erase that.

These men I have written about were all, in a manner of speaking, on the run, and I felt moved to ask who and what they were running from. There are CEOs, gamers, whiz kids, Silicon Valley entrepreneurs who thrive via the Internet, and they are not outlaws, and their story of the Internet would be very different. But I found men who are ghosts in the gleaming machine and who raise a question or two.

One of a writer's rewards is to find himself alive in the detail of his stories, and the Age of the Internet provides a whole new funfair of existential provocations. In my childhood the visiting funfair was called "the Shows," and that is how I think of these tales, as bulletins from the edge of modern selfhood, where a few carnivalesque men are bent out of shape—by their pasts, by their ambitions, or by their illusions—under the Internet's big tent. In a world where everybody can be anybody, where being real is no big deal, I wanted to work back to the human problems, and that is what drives these stories, the sense that our computers are not yet ourselves. In a hall of mirrors we only seem like someone else.

Ghosting

O n January 5, 2011, at 8:30 p.m., I was messing about at home when the phone buzzed on the sofa. It was a text from Jamie Byng, the publisher of Canongate. "Are you about?" it said. "I have a somewhat left-field idea. It's potentially very exciting. But I need to discuss urgently." Canongate had bought, for £600,000, a memoir by the WikiLeaks founder, Julian Assange. The book had also been bought for a high sum by Sonny Mehta at Knopf in New York, and Jamie had sold foreign rights to a slew of big houses. He said he expected it to be published in forty languages. Assange didn't want to write the book himself and he hoped the book's ghostwriter could be somebody who didn't already know a lot about him. I told Jamie that I'd seen Assange in London at the Frontline Club, a watering hole for foreign correspondents, the year before, when the first WikiLeaks released its first stories, and that he was really interesting but odd, maybe even on the autism spectrum. Jamie agreed, but said it was an amazing story. "He wants a kind of manifesto, a book that will reflect this great big generational shift." He'd been to see Assange in Norfolk and was going again the next day. He said he and the agent Caroline Michel had suggested me for the job and that Assange wanted to meet me. I knew they'd been talking to other writers, and I was at first skeptical.

It's not unusual for published writers to get requests to write things anonymously. How much did Alex Haley protect Malcolm X when he ghosted his autobiography? To what extent did Ted Sorensen create the verbal manner of John F. Kennedy when he wrote *Profiles in Courage*, a book for which the future president won the Pulitzer Prize? And are the science fiction stories H. P. Lovecraft ghosted for Harry Houdini not the best things he ever wrote? There would be a touch of all this in the strange case of Assange. But there is something else about the genre, a sense that the world might be more ghosted now than at any time in history. Isn't Wikipedia entirely ghosted? Isn't half of Facebook? Isn't the World Wide Web a new ether, in which we are all haunted by ghostwriters?

I had written about missing persons and celebrity, about secrecy and conflict, and I knew from the start that this story might be an insider's job. However it came, and however I unearthed it or inflected it, the Assange story would be consistent with my instinct to walk the unstable border between fiction and nonfiction, to see how porous the parameters between invention and personality are. I remembered Victor Maskell, the art historian and spy in John Banville's *The Untouchable*, who liked to quote Diderot: "We erect a statue in our own image inside ourselves—idealised, you know, but still recognisable—and then spend our lives engaged in the effort to make ourselves into its likeness." The fact that the WikiLeaks story was playing out against a global argument over privacy, secrets, and the abuse of military power left me feeling the story might be irresistible.

At 5:30 the next evening Jamie arrived at my flat with his editorial colleague Nick Davies. (Mental health warning: there are two people named Nick Davies in this story. This one worked for Canongate; the second is a well-known reporter for *The Guardian*.) They had just come back on the train from Norfolk. Jamie said that Assange had accidentally poked his eye with a log or something, so had sat through three hours of discussion with his eyes closed. They were going to advertise the book for April. It was to be called *WikiLeaks Versus the World: My Story* by Julian Assange. They said I would have a percentage of the royalties in every territory and Julian was happy with that. We talked about the deal and then Jamie went into detail about the security issues. "Are you ready to have your phone tapped by the CIA?" he asked. He said Julian insisted the book would have to be written on a laptop that had no Internet access.

When I arrived at Ellingham Hall a few days later Assange was fast asleep. He'd been living there, at the house of Vaughan Smith, one of his guarantors and founder of the Frontline Club, since his arrest on Swedish rape allegations. He was effectively under house arrest and wearing an electronic tag on his leg. He would sign in at Beccles police station every afternoon, proving he hadn't done a runner in the night. Assange and his associates kept hackers' hours: up all night and asleep half the day, one of the little bits of chaos that would come to characterize the circus I was about to enter. Ellingham Hall is a drafty country residence with stags' heads in the hall. In the dining room there were laptops everywhere. Sarah Harrison, Assange's personal assistant and girlfriend, was wearing a woolly jumper and kept scraping her ringlets off her face. Another girl, maybe Spanish or South American or Eastern European, came into the drawing room, where the fire was blazing. I stood at the windows looking at the tall trees outside.

Sarah made me a cup of tea and the other girl brought it into the room with a plate of chocolate biscuits. "I'm always trying to think of new ways to wake him up," she said. "The cleaner just barges in. It's the only way." He soon came padding into the room in socks and a suit.

"I'm sorry I'm late," he said. He was amused and suspicious at the same time, a nice combination, I thought, and there were few signs of the mad unprofessionalism to come. He said the thing that worried him was how quickly the book had to be written. It would be hard to establish a structure that would work. He went on to say that he might be in jail soon and that might not be bad for writing the book. "I have quite abstract thoughts," he said, "and an argument about civilization and secrecy that needs to be got down."

He said he'd hoped to have something that read like Hemingway. "When people have been put in prison who might never have had time to write, the thing they write can be galvanizing and amazing. I wouldn't say this publicly, but Hitler wrote *Mein Kampf* in prison." He admitted it wasn't a great book but it wouldn't have been written if Hitler had not been put away. He said that Tim Geithner, the U.S. secretary of the treasury, had been asked to look into ways to hinder companies that would profit from subversive organizations. That meant Knopf would come under fire for publishing the book.

I asked him if he had a working title yet, and he said, to laughter, "Yes. *Ban This Book: From Swedish Whores to Pentagon Bores.*" It was interesting to see how he parried with some notion of himself as a public figure, as a rock star, really, when all the activists I've ever known tend to see themselves as marginal and possibly eccentric figures. Assange referred a number of times to the fact that people were in love with him, but I couldn't see the coolness, the charisma he took for granted. He spoke at length about his "enemies," mainly *The Guardian* and *The New York Times*.

Julian's relationship with *The Guardian*, which appeared to obsess him, went back to his original agreement to let them publish material that WikiLeaks had procured, it turned out, from Bradley (now Chelsea) Manning, a giant cache of coalition war logs that gave details of military incidents in Afghanistan. Julian quickly fell out with the journalists and editors at *The Guardian*—essentially over questions of power and ownership—and by the time I took up with him felt "double-crossed" by them. It was an early sign of the way he viewed "collaboration": *The Guardian* was an enemy because he'd "given" them something and they hadn't toed the line, whereas the *Daily Mail* was almost respected for finding him entirely abominable. *The Guardian* tried to soothe him—its editor then, Alan Rusbridger, showed concern for his position, as did his deputy, Ian Katz, and others—but he talked about its journalists in savage terms. *The Guardian* felt strongly that the secret material ought to be redacted to protect informants or bystanders named in it, and Julian was inconsistent about that. I never believed he wanted to endanger such people, but he chose to interpret *The Guardian*'s concern as "cowardice."

His relationship with *The New York Times* was every bit as toxic. He believed its editor at the time, Bill Keller, was determined to treat him as a "source" rather than a collaborator—which was true—and that Keller wanted to hang him out to dry, which was not true. Keller wrote a long piece in his own paper saying Julian was dirty, paranoid, controlling, unreliable, and slightly off his head, which naturally made Julian feel his former collaborator was out to get him. But both newspapers, in concert with others, had given over vast numbers of pages to the leaks and given WikiLeaks top billing in bringing the material to light. I always felt the involvement of *The New York Times* would save Julian from prison, and I still believe that. Even the U.S. authorities know that it would be impossible for them to convict Assange of espionage without also convicting Keller and Rusbridger. But instead of seeing that, Julian could only view the men in personal terms as dissemblers or something worse.

He had a strange inability to realize when he was becoming

boring or demanding. He talked as if the world needed him to talk and never to stop. Oddly for a dissident, he had no questions. The left wingers I have known are always full of questions, but Assange, from the first, seemed like a manifestation of the hyperventilating chat room. It became clear: if I was to be the ghost, it might turn out that I was the least ghostly person in the enterprise.

He was avoiding "our book." He wanted to discuss the other books about to be published. "There's this book by two guys from *Der Spiegel*," he said. "It will be more high-toned than the others. The two guys are friendly towards me but the book will contain new allegations." He spoke about another book to be published by *The Guardian*. He said it would come from journalists he'd worked with there. He was obsessed with David Leigh and Nick Davies, two of the main reporters. "Davies is extremely hostile to me," Assange said. "*The Guardian* basically double-crossed the organization in the worst way . . . We left them with a cache of cables—to act as security in case any of us got it in the neck—and they made a copy of the data. They were against my getting other media organizations involved, so they leaked the data to *The New York Times* and others and they behaved abominably. Davies has a known personal animosity towards me." (*The Guardian* denies all this.)

"Why?"

"Because he's an old man who's basically at the end of his career. He can't bear it that a onetime source of advancement has gone away. He wrote a smear about me and none of the *Guardian* management stood in his way." He mentioned Ian Katz as failing in this regard. He said *The Guardian*'s behavior would likely be laid out in *Der Spiegel*'s book, and that the *Guardian* journalists were obviously keen to put out their version. "They have scheduled the book to come out at the time of my legal hearing, to cause maximum damage."

"Surely not," I said, incredulous. "Wouldn't they wait, just for old times' sake?"

"You're joking."

He said the third book was by his former colleague Daniel Domscheit-Berg. "This will be a complete smear," he said. "The guy is working from hatred of us and he will seek to make it as damaging as possible."

"Embarrassing or damaging?"

"Both, probably. He has chat room stuff . . . conversations."

"Between all of you?"

"Yes," he said. "He put out one of them before, about having been suspended. He printed all the stuff in the conversation except the parts that related to why he was suspended. There is also a book by the *New York Times* journalists and several other quick books. But these will be damaging, too, because they will just repeat the worst allegations."

I'd never been with a person who had such a good cause and such a poor ear, nor had I met a head of an organization with such an unending capacity to worry about his enemies and to yawn in one's face. I asked him how he thought the court case would turn out. "I have, I'd say, a forty percent chance of being freed," he said. "If they free me on February 6, I'll leave the country immediately because in this country there would be a second arrest and the U.S. will be determined to have me extradited. I would sooner be in a country where no extradition treaty exists with the U.S., such as Cuba or Switzerland. A lot of people in America want me dead and there was an article in *The Washington Times* which showed my face with a target on it and blood coming out the back of my head."

He suggested I come with him to the police station at Beccles. We went outside and waited for Sarah to get the car. Standing there, I saw that the contradictions might just work out well for the book. I saw he had problems but he could be funny and I liked him. Ellingham Hall is surrounded by barns and storage buildings. "I would like to convert one of those stables into an office," he said. He smiled. "And a book was born in a manger."

"You'd never find three wise men and a virgin in Norfolk," I said. He made another joke about Norfolk, about local social workers stamping cases N.F.N.—"Normal for Norfolk." He phoned ahead to the police station to tell them he was coming. There were two phones on his lap but he answered neither one himself. A French journalist was following the car but lost us. At the police station, Sarah stopped and said: "Shall I do the honors?" I watched as she went out and searched the bushes.

"Is she checking for paparazzi?" I asked.

"I wish," said Julian.

"What, then?"

"Assassins."

I said I would write the book on condition that I could do it without being named, for the thrill of getting the story right and learning something in the process. I thought I would have a kind of authorly freedom by not being the author on the cover. I told Jamie I didn't want my name anywhere on the book and that I wouldn't give interviews or talk about the project. I wouldn't become a WikiLeaks spokesman or go on *Newsnight* or confirm anything with the newspapers. I wanted to let the publication speak for itself. I was assured this would work and Julian agreed.

On Monday, January 17, 2011, I drove to Norfolk. It was dark and drizzly by the time I got to Ellingham Hall. I stopped the car and got changed in a lane, putting a hoodie over a T-shirt, while rabbits hopped in the headlamps. I'd been told there were journalists everywhere, and indeed there were lights around the fields and sometimes helicopters overhead. I looked at the driveway under a full moon. It felt almost comically filmic, a strange technological distortion of Jane Austen's novels, with character and power waiting to combust. The house loomed through the fog, as they say, and I texted Sarah to say I was two minutes away from the door.

The kitchen was the usual thing: blue Aga stove, double sink, farmhouse table, plates everywhere. On top of the Aga a garlic loaf was warming and on the table was a little bowl of tomato salad. I could hear American voices through the door that led to the drawing room, and one Australian voice, Julian's. On the walls of the dining room there were many paintings hung on brass rails. One of them showed a nineteenth-century gentleman. I later found out he was Vaughan Smith's ancestor who had expanded the estate after marrying into it. Vaughan's father was ruddy-faced and in uniform. Julian later told me the white thing he was holding was a diplomatic bag.

Filming was going on. There was always filming or the possibility of filming, which was odd for people who liked to think of themselves as hiding in the shadows. "You want a book to read?" Sarah asked. "I've got tons of your books upstairs." The television people were from the U.S. show *60 Minutes* and were making a film about WikiLeaks. I heard Julian say to them that this was his gilded cage, the same thing he had said to me several days earlier. While Julian continued to deal with the interviewer in the drawing room, Sarah and I had a drink in the kitchen. She said she was from South London and had come to work for the organization the previous July. She brought up the rape allegations and said they were "the most massive cliché." "We expected flak from the Pentagon," she said, "but not smears based on two weeks in Sweden." She said it was bizarre what the Swedes considered to be rape, yet some of her friends were distressed by the allegations and couldn't believe she would work for WikiLeaks. She also said she thought the allegations were mad. She asked me about my career and we spoke about the writing business. "I thought I'd get to do a lot of traveling in this job," she said, laughing, "but instead I've been stuck in one house in the English countryside since last October."

We sat down to dinner at ten. Vaughan joined us, pulling baked potatoes out of the oven and lasagne that had been prepared by the housekeeper. We had a joking conversation about movie rights in general and they all larked about who should play them in the movie. Vaughan was most concerned about the movie company hiring the house for filming. I told them about Battle Bridge Road, the place in King's Cross where I lived in my twenties, which was used all the time as a film set. I told them about the day they were making a film about Oswald Mosley and staging a riot in our street. The hippies who squatted nearby thought the revolution had begun and ran out and joined the fray. "Who's Mosley?" Julian asked.

When we began speaking about the book, I was concerned to get a sense of what the elements were, so that I could think about how to build the picture. I said that perhaps there should be a narrative in which the past and present alternated. "What did you think of *Anna Karenina*?" Assange said. "I just thought it took too much of my life away. But then there's this scene where the dog begins to speak, and I thought, yes, this is beginning to make sense."

The biggest surprise for readers of his book, I suggested, would be to discover it wasn't written luridly or defensively but quite frankly.

"Maybe it should be experimental," he said, "like chapter one has one word; chapter two has two words . . ."

"The real innovation," I said, "would be to come up with a book that sums up the relationship between the individual and the state as it seems from your position now."

"But I am not a complete person yet," he said.

"It will be the book you can write now."

He wanted his book to be like Thomas Paine's *Rights of Man*.

I noticed he tended to eat pretty much with his hands. People in magazine articles say he doesn't eat, but he had three helpings of lasagne that night and he ate both the baked potato and the jam pudding with his hands. He turned from being very open and engaged to being removed and sort of disgusted. About midnight, he and Sarah, while continuing to talk, lifted over their MacBooks and opened them and began to type with their faces strangely lit. After a while, Sarah exclaimed.

"What?" I asked.

"Bloody hell." She looked at Assange.

"What?" he asked.

"*The Guardian* have redacted the following from a cable about Tunisia," she said.

"Read what they've redacted," said Julian.

She read two sentences about a deposed president having sought cancer treatment abroad. "They're taking them out," she said.

Julian made a face. "They're disgusting."

"Why do it?" Sarah asked. Julian said they were obviously worried about being sued.

"Come on," Sarah said.

Julian: "British courts."

Julian always behaved as if he was being pushed onto the back foot over redactions.

The issue was this: on July 28, 2010, Major General Campbell, a U.S. commander in Afghanistan, said, "Any time there's any sort of leak of classified material, it has the potential to harm the military folks that are working out here every day." The notion got under the skin of many people, including some of the journalists dealing with the leaks, and a feeling grew among the "media partners" and many supporters of the organization that WikiLeaks must avoid having "blood on its hands." Julian gave several answers to the question of how the leaked material should be "redacted." Sometimes he appeared to suggest that editing it was wrong, but he admitted to me that they wanted to "improve when it came to having a better focus on redactions." He denied ever saying, as reported by others, that informants' names should not be taken out and that "they deserved to die." He would go over these positions again and again, but the interviews I conducted contain many inconsistencies. And horrible longueurs.

At ten o'clock one night I drove over to the house and Julian spoke for nearly three hours without pause. At one point he looked quite moved as he spoke about "backstabbers." He talked about Domscheit-Berg. In some way he found it impossible to imagine how other people could have a view of him, or of themselves, that didn't accord with his own. "Every good story needs a Judas," he said, and "nearly everybody is a fucking wanker." He spoke about other people he'd worked with, and felt it would be different with me. (I was never certain it would be, though I hoped so.) "You are in artistic control of this book," he said. I replied that I felt the book could become an argument about disclosure, about the difference between secrets of a political kind, on the one hand, and the tabloid hunt for salacious details about private lives, on the other. The book, I said, should be revealing on all fronts, but also be frank about revelation itself. If he could not discuss a matter of importance—his son, for example, and the custody battle, or what happened in bed with the two Swedish girls—we should seek to explain why in a statement about sleaze. I said what we shouldn't do was close our eyes and hope no one would notice. Making the ends meet in a moral sense was the project's great conundrum, and he agreed at that point to let me say everything, in the spirit of just saying what happened.

On Wednesday, January 19, it rained all day. I was beginning to wonder about the time-wasting. I couldn't understand the slow and lazy way they went about things. They always talked about the pressure of work, about how busy they were, but, compared with most journalists, they sat on their arses half the day. Julian's favorite activity was following what people—especially his "enemies"—were saying about him on the Internet. When I told him I'd sooner cut my balls off than google myself, he found a high-minded reason for explaining why it was important for him to know what other people were saying.

That night, a guy from Al Jazeera was talking to the group. The group was usually just Sarah, who lived there, and Joseph Farrell, a pleasant twentysomething whiz kid who came and went. Another guy, an activist and academic from Canberra University, was drinking wine and talking about how to mobilize the world. It turned out that the guy from Al Jazeera was hoping to strike a deal with WikiLeaks—that's to say, with Julian. He was offering $1.3 million to get access (via encryption keys) to the data. He also wanted to organize a conference in Qatar on press freedom. There were Russian cigarettes on the table and everyone took turns to go outside and smoke. Julian was on cigars. Sarah did a lot of the negotiating over the Al Jazeera deal—it got quite heated at one point—but Julian would intervene, and in the end everything was signed, though I have no knowledge if the money was actually paid or if any of the material was used by Al Jazeera. The man from Canberra was telling everyone they should have links with the new anarchists in Paris, who had the lowdown on how badly the French government had behaved in relation to the former colonies. "It would be good to do better in France," Julian said.

Kristinn Hrafnsson, an Icelandic investigative reporter and WikiLeaks spokesman—who appeared to have survived Julian's many culls of his old friends—was sitting next to me with his laptop open. He turned it to show an e-mail from David Leigh of *The Guardian*. Someone said Leigh had just been quoted in *Vanity Fair* saying that Assange was "out of money and out of leaks." The e-mail from Leigh was asking for two clarifications for his book. One was to do with a dating website Assange was once a member of. And the second was a question about the identity of his father. At the close of the e-mail, Leigh said he wanted to be "fair-minded" and said that he really meant it.

"What a sleazy cocksucker," Julian said. "Who does he think he's talking to?" It wasn't the first time I noticed how deeply adversarial WikiLeaks was in its relationship with its friends. Julian treated his supporters as subjects, and learned nothing when they walked away. He hardly mentioned the right-wing press that called him a criminal and a traitor: he expended all his ire on the journalists who had tried to work with him and who had basic sympathy for his political position. In a bank safe, I have dozens of hours of taped interviews with Assange in which he rails maniacally against *The Guardian* and *The New York Times*. He would go into these interminable, Herzog-like monologues, and, after many of these long nights, I would wonder if the job wasn't getting closer to fiction than I'd suspected. Before my eyes, and with no regard for me or my tape recorder, he snapped the olive branch proffered by those he hated.

I picked up my papers and went into the dining room with Julian. After a little while, Sarah joined us. I wanted to discuss the book's structure. Julian said we should consider having a chapter called "Women."

"I thought this was going to be like a manifesto," Sarah said.

Julian bristled slightly. They were a proper couple: flirting and fighting and not-saying. "It is," he said, "but with personal history woven through."

"I just think . . ."

"Don't worry about it."

"Just . . ."

"Don't worry."

She turned to me. "He's got such appalling, sleazy stories about women you wouldn't believe it. I don't want to hear all that."

"Hold on," he said.

"No. Sorry. I don't think that's what the book's about, your stories of sleeping with women."

He wanted again to discuss Nick Davies, the *Guardian* reporter who had worked with him on the initial newspaper deal to publish the leaks. "The problem was he was in love with me," said Julian. "Not sexually. But just in love with me. Like I was this younger guy he wanted to be." He said the same thing about the Icelandic politician and activist Birgitta Jónsdóttir: "She was in love with me." I knew from then on that any understanding of him would involve a recognition of his narcissism. "I went to the local pub," he said, "and the people in the bar were gossiping about me, while I was there. One of them said: 'The local ladies will be pleased.'"

"Did you miss me?" Julian asked when I came back from a spell in London. He was eating two bars of Violet Crumble (a honeycomb chocolate bar). I said there'd been speculation in the press about my involvement with him, that it was quite difficult, I'd known a lot of these people for years, they were friends, and not answering e-mails or confirming stories was tough.

"Well, you could just come out in support of me," Julian said.

"That's not the deal," I said. "I'm anonymous. There's no point in this otherwise."

Sarah was clicking on her laptop. "That's quite good," she said. "I've got you twenty thousand pounds for doing an hour's interview by Skype." It was for some group of company presidents.

"That's not much," Julian said.

"Ingratitude."

"Well," Julian said, "if Tony Blair—a war criminal—can get one hundred and twenty thousand, I should get at least one pound more than him."

"You want me to write back to them and say you want more money?"

"Yes," said Julian.

Later, Julian was on the phone trying to instruct Alan Dershowitz—"The ultra-Zionist American lawyer"—to represent WikiLeaks in its fight with the U.S. federal government over the government's attempt to subpoena the organization's Twitter account. "It's good politics to get him," Julian said. "Even if we lose him later. The middle-right-wing faction in America will respond to him fighting on our behalf."

I looked in the visitors' book at Ellingham Hall. Under November 29, 2010, Julian had signed his name and written a message: "Today with my friends we tried to bring modern history to the world." It was the day after WikiLeaks began publishing

251,287 leaked U.S. embassy cables, the largest set of confidential documents ever released into the public domain. I wanted to get a lot of his childhood stuff down but he spent the night going off his head about the forthcoming edition of the BBC's weekly current affairs program *Panorama*. It seems the reporter John Sweeney had put together "a swingeing attack." Julian flames up when confronted with stuff like this.

Another afternoon, I was trying to get him to stop his undergraduate lecturing about freedom. I knew there was nothing I could use: it was all standard-grade Voltaire with a smattering of Chomsky. Sarah came in with a couple of FedEx boxes. A few weeks earlier, the billionaire (and Jimmy Choo–associated financier) Matthew Mellon, for whom Julian was a hero, had landed his helicopter in the field outside the house and come in to have lunch. He said it was a pity a CEO such as Julian only really had one suit. Mellon said he would send him some clothes in the post. They'd forgotten about it until the FedEx boxes appeared. "Oh my God," Sarah said, "they're actually in here."

There were two suits by Ozwald Boateng, a white shirt from Turnbull & Asser, and a couple of ties, both from the gift shop at the Metropolitan Museum of Art. The suits had bright linings, one pomegranate-colored, the other aqua. I told Julian that Boateng was the famous black British suit-maker of Savile Row. "That's great," he said. "It fits the blaxploitation theme I'm hoping for with the film of my life. I want Morgan Freeman to play me." He began stripping off and I saw he had a pair of Tesco's trackie bottoms under his old suit. He donned each suit in turn and asked us to tell him how he looked. He was anxious to know if they fitted properly. "Isn't this one a bit baggy on the arse?" he asked. I looked at the note Matthew Mellon had sent. "Julian: Hope this finds you well. Some Savile Row suits I thought you might find useful. Hopefully there is a Taylar [*sic*] nearby . . . All the best to you and the gang."

I spoke to Jamie Byng, who made the point that Julian didn't appear to see how unattractive he could seem. He said the book would fail if we didn't know how to temper or transform that, if the book didn't save him from himself and go deeper than his defenses. I knew what he meant. I told him I was trying to give Julian a crash course in self-deprecation, and would continue to insist that he not make himself the hero of every anecdote. I told Jamie the work WikiLeaks was trying to do might be bigger than Julian's ability to articulate it.

There was this incredible need for spy talk. Julian would often refer to the places where he lived as "safe houses" and say things such as "When you go to Queensland there's a contact there you should speak to."

"You mean a friend?" I'd say.

"No. It's more complicated than that." He appeared to like the notion that he was being pursued, and the tendency was only complicated by the fact that there were real pursuers. But the pursuit was never as grave as he wanted it to be. He stuck to his Cold War tropes, where one didn't deliver a package but made a "drop-off." One day, we were due to meet some of the WikiLeaks staff at a farmhouse out toward Lowestoft. We went in my car. Julian was especially edgy that afternoon, feeling perhaps that the walls were closing in, as we bumped down one of those flat roads covered in muck left by tractor tires. "Quick, quick," he said, "go left. We're being followed!" I looked in the rearview mirror and could see a white Mondeo with a wire sticking out the back.

"Don't be daft, Julian," I said. "That's a taxi."

"No. Listen to me. It's surveillance. We're being followed. Quickly go left." Just by comical chance, as I was rocking a *Starsky and Hutch*–style handbrake turn, the car behind us suddenly stopped at a farmhouse gate and a little boy jumped out and ran up the path. I looked at the clock as we rolled off in a cloud of dust. It said 3:48.

"That was a kid being delivered home from school," I said. "You're mental."

"You don't understand," he said.

There was plenty of laughter at the table in Ellingham Hall, followed by long periods of boredom. The laughter had a lot to do with Sarah, who had a nice way of teasing Julian, and a lot to do with the man himself, who responds well to jokes. It was all part of that discontented winter, when the book kept sliding back on itself. On a good day, it was inspiring to see them go after some lying politician or some corrupt tin-pot government. It was exciting to think, in that very Jane Austen kind of house, that no novel had ever captured this new sort of history, where military lies on a global scale were revealed by a bunch of sleepy amateurs two feet from an Aga stove.

Eventually, I found a house to rent in Bungay, ten minutes away from Ellingham Hall, a place to work quietly and get away from the general stagnation. I was driving a lot and trying to find a way into the book, but the delaying tactics on Julian's part had become insane. When I tried to talk to him about dates, he talked about his forthcoming trial hearing and told me Fidel Castro had sent a message to say WikiLeaks was the only website he liked. The *60 Minutes* program went out in America and the response was massive. One commentator said Julian should be awarded the Nobel Peace Prize; another said he had set back the cause of democracy by decades. In the midst of all the kitchen chaos, Julian puffed a cigar and I was reminded, as if I needed reminding, that nobody is simply one thing: history was full of messy characters exercising their rudeness and eating with their hands while changing the world. I tried to keep that in mind as the days passed. "In one fell swoop," said *Foreign Policy*, "the candor of the cables released by WikiLeaks did more for Arab democracy than decades of backstage US diplomacy."

One of the things Julian found it hardest to admit to was the amount of hacking he did himself. He had worked out that being an "editor" was somehow a necessary front for much that he did. He objected to the idea that WikiLeaks "stole" secrets: according to him they simply understood, at a deeply sophisticated level, how the flow of information in society could be altered. Far from being a slave to machines, he doubted their morality, feeling that computers were already being used all over the world to control us, and that only the moral and the wise and the fleet of finger, such as those at WikiLeaks, had the requisite understanding to fight back. In 2011, during the Egyptian uprising, Hosni Mubarak tried to close down the country's mobile-phone network, a service that came through the Canadian telecom company Nortel. Julian and his gang gained access to Nortel's servers and fought against Mubarak's official hackers to reverse the process. The revolution continued and Julian was satisfied, sitting back in our remote kitchen eating chocolates.

That is why I didn't walk out. The story was just too large. What Julian lacked in efficiency or professionalism he made up for in courage. What he lacked in carefulness he made up for in impact. In our overnight conversations, he told me about the mind-set of the expert hacker. He described how, as a teenager, he'd wandered through the virtual corridors of NASA, Bank of America, the Melbourne transport system, and the Pentagon. At his best, he represented a new way of existing in relation to authority. He wasn't very straightforwardly of the left and couldn't have distinguished dialectical materialism from a bag of nuts. He hates systems of belief, hates all systems, wants indeed to be a ghost in the machine, walking through the corridors of power and switching off the lights. I found myself writing notes culled from what he said to me about himself. "When you're a hacker you're interested in masks within masks" and "We could undermine corruption from its dead center. Justice will always in the end be about human beings, but there is a new vanguard of experts, criminalized as we are, who have fastened onto the cancer of modern power, and seen how it spreads in ways that are still hidden from ordinary human experience."

But he was also losing touch with promises he had made and contracts he'd signed. His paranoia was losing him support, and in a normal organization, one where other people's experience was respected and where their value was judged on more than "loyalty," he would have been fired. I would have fired him myself if I hadn't been there merely to help him put words to his ideas. But his sentences, too, were infected with his habits of self-regard and truth manipulation. The man who put himself in charge of disclosing the world's secrets simply couldn't bear his own. The story of his life mortified him and sent him scurrying for excuses. He didn't want to do the book. He hadn't from the beginning.

I sat back and watched. The night of Sarah's birthday there was champagne and jokes, but it ended with Julian and Sarah poring over the WikiLeaks book written by the two *Guardian* journalists David Leigh and Luke Harding, which had been published that day. Sarah would read out the "bad bits," and he would say "It's disgusting" or "That's malicious libel." I thought it was all quite lowering, the book's interest in his sex life and their interest in the book's interest. "It says here you carried abortion pills around with you that were really just sugar pills."

Julian: "What?"

Sarah: "And that you set out to impregnate girls. It says you said to one of them you would call her baby Afghanistan. Well, that does sound like you. I've heard you say that sort of thing, about naming babies after your campaigns. But you wouldn't leave all these girls to have babies on their own, would you?"

Julian: "Sarah."

Sarah: "I'm just asking. Have you been at the births of all your children?"

Julian: "All except one."

But I thought he only had one son? Was he lying to me about his life? He started following Leigh's Twitter feed and I saw, over his shoulder, many of the replies he was making on WikiLeaks's behalf. I could see he thought I was bonkers not to think *The Guardian* a force of evil. "You don't understand the extent of the problem," he would say. But I believe I understood it all too well.

"Is this a good use of our time?" I said it again and again and it had no impact. One of his strategies was to invent, on the spot, new avant-garde styles that the book should adopt. One day he said the book should contain parables and he suggested the paragraphs should be numbered, like verses. "You've got to get yourself and your staff to see the book as a priority," I said. "A great book will set things right. It will constitute a much bigger thing than turf wars or tweets."

"But it can't be the priority," Julian said. "Ending wars and starting a revolution in Libya is the priority."

He started coming to the house in Bungay every day. I'd make lunch, waiting for him to get off the phone or stop ranting about Mark Stephens, his lawyer. Sometimes he was ranting *at* Stephens, and I have a tape where you can hear each side of the conversation as they talk about money. During those days at the Bungay house I would try to sit him down with a new list of questions, and he'd shy away from them, saying he wasn't in the mood or there were more pressing matters to deal with. I think he was just keen to get away from Ellingham Hall. I had the Internet. I made lunch every day and he'd eat it, often with his hands, and then lick the plate. In all that time he didn't once take his dirty plate to the sink. That doesn't make him like Josef Mengele, but, you know, life is life.

I wasn't only struggling to get him to commit to the book, I was struggling to keep the project dark. I didn't answer any of the calls I received from the press. There was clearly a leak, which is poetic justice, I suppose, when you're working with WikiLeaks.

Julian came up to London for the appeal hearing on Sunday, February 6, 2011. At midnight I went over to the house he was staying at in Southwick Mews in Paddington. The house was Vaughan's office, near the Frontline Club, and was full of office equipment; a large conference room was filled with "friends" of WikiLeaks. I went up to a small bedroom at the top of the house and found Julian lying on an unmade bed. There were clothes on the floor and books about Internet amateurs on the nightstand, along with David Remnick's book on Barack Obama. Julian was cutting his nails. "Do you know why I'm doing this, cutting my nails?" he asked.

"Nope."

"So the court doesn't look at my nails and think they are the nails of someone who rips condoms"—one of the Swedish women had alleged that he had ripped off a condom during sex. Like everyone else, the Swedish women were merely figures passing by on the other side of the glass.

A group of pro-WikiLeaks protesters were lined up outside Belmarsh courthouse. They stood behind fences and began to cheer when we arrived. Julian was wearing one of the Boateng suits but the effect wasn't great because he insisted on wearing a gray duffel coat on top. We went upstairs to the consultation room and everybody seemed to be there. The lawyers were headed by Stephens, an ebullient, red-faced mucker straight out of Dickens, saturated in media savvy. He stood among the sureties and supporters: the Socialist MP Tony Benn, the activist and heiress Jemima Khan, Bianca Jagger, the author James Fox and the fashion designer Bella Freud, and the five or so young people I associated with WikiLeaks. We were led up to seats in the gallery they'd saved for friends. As soon as I sat and looked down at the court I saw Esther Addley of *The Guardian*. She saw me and smiled, and I smiled back and she lifted her BlackBerry. "Tweeting," I thought, and, sure enough, within minutes she tweeted that I had come in with the Assange party. "Rumoured ghostwriter. Rumour confirmed?" she wrote.

The well-known barrister Geoffrey Robertson, for Assange, argued that the person in Sweden who issued the warrant, Marianne Ny, was not, as she described herself, the "chief prosecutor" but a minor prosecutor not qualified to do what she did. This seemed weak to me. I also wondered whether Mr. Justice Riddle would feel antagonized by Robertson's seeming upper-class snobbery. Julian sat behind glass in the dock and joked with the guards. Sarah was sitting beside me and pretty much slept for two hours. At lunchtime, I headed home and then reappeared at the mews at midnight. Julian was lying on the bed again, going over the day's events while Sarah cut his hair with a pair of fairly blunt-looking scissors. He was critical of Robertson's opening. "He failed to go for the heart before going for the head," Julian said. "And I wasn't happy with him not using the words 'beyond reasonable doubt' enough." Sarah opened a box of Ferrero Rocher and we lay on the bed discussing it all. I repeated the phrase I'd used weeks before when I talked to Jamie Byng: "I want to give you a crash course in self-deprecation." He said he had been far more self-deprecating before the custody battle for his son, which damaged him.

Sometime in the early hours, he showed me a webpage. It said: "Assange Kept Touching My Pussy, Says Ex-WikiLeaker." He was chortling like mad. It was a story from the Domscheit-Berg book *Inside WikiLeaks*, which told how Assange was always trying to control everything, including Domscheit-Berg's cat, which, the book alleged, Julian kept strangling in a playful way.

People turned up out of nowhere. No one introduced them properly, and they didn't have surnames anyway: they were just Carlos or Tina or Oliver or Thomas. One night in Ellingham Hall, a French guy called Jeremy came in with a sack of encrypted phones. Julian always seemed to have three phones on the go at any one time—the red phone was his personal one—and this latest batch was designed to deal with a general paranoia that newspapers were hacking all of us. It was always like that: sudden bursts of vigilance would vie with complete negligence. There was no real system of security or applied secrecy, not if you've read about how spy agencies operate. Julian would speak on open lines when he simply forgot to take care. The others kept the same mobile phones for months. And none of them seemed to care about a running tape recorder. Granted, I was there to ask questions and record replies, but still, much of what they said had nothing to do with the book and they simply forgot about it. Only once was I asked to sign a confidentiality agreement, when Julian gave me a hard drive containing very sensitive material, but they forgot I had the drive and never asked for it back.

He's not a details guy. None of them are. What they love is the big picture and the general fight. They love the noise and the glamour, the history, the spectacle, but not the fine print. That is why they released so many cables so quickly: for impact. And there's a good argument to support that. But, even today, years later, the cables have never had the dedicated attention they deserve. They made a splash and then were left languishing. We saw this love of spectacle and lack of detailed thinking more recently, during the 2016 U.S. presidential election, when Assange, keen to do anything to express his apparent hatred of Hillary Clinton, allowed his organization to be aligned with the work of Russian hackers, who were feeding him leaks from the Democratic National Committee. A more thoughtful editor, less narcissistic and not so desperate for a quick impact, would have weighed the "gain" of disgracing Clinton against the danger of helping Trump, and he would have avoided being seen to meddle in the democratic process of a foreign nation and ally himself with Putin's authoritarian regime. Assange has no self-control and no sense of basic public relations, and his attempt to bend the American election harmed him in every way it is possible for a "freedom-fighting" journalist to be harmed. Officials at the Ecuadorian embassy, where he lived in conditions of asylum, temporarily cut off his Internet access—but to Assange it was all worth it because it allowed him to get back at an old enemy. Perhaps it also allowed him to feel relevant, at a time when many of his former supporters felt his hubris had driven WikiLeaks into the ground. After the release of the diplomatic cables of 2011, I always hoped someone would do a serious editing job, ordering them country by country, contextualizing each one, providing a proper introduction, detailing each injustice and each breach, but Julian wanted the next splash and, even more, he wanted to scrap with each critic he found on the Internet. As for the book, he kept putting it off.

Carelessness is a "tell." For months, Julian thought he was in control of his relationship with his publishers, agent, lawyers, and writer, but he was demonstrating every day in a hundred ways that he couldn't face the book. He'd signed up for it, he was pretending to work on it, but, even before he let the whole thing run out of control, he was dignifying his denial with higher appointments and legal struggles. The book became his evil "other," his nightmare autobiography, and rather than being haunted by me, his ghost, he decided to convert me into a quietly ineffective follower. In a moment of helpfulness, he asked his mother to send a load of photographs from his childhood. He gave me the disk and completely forgot about it.

Julian lost the appeal against extradition and promptly lodged a further appeal. It was ordained that he would continue at Ellingham Hall. I'd been in Australia doing some writers' festivals, and when I got back there was a different atmosphere in Norfolk. I'd always been amazed at how Vaughan Smith and his family had been able to cope with the whole studenty WikiLeaks caravan in their house—the Smiths have young children—with its all-night rituals and almost comically bad table manners. Julian had a way of making himself, in his own eyes, impervious to the small matters that might detain others. If you told him to do the dishes he would say he was trying to free economic slaves in China and had no time to wash up. He stood at the center of a little amateur empire, and any professional incursions, from lawyers, from filmmakers, from publishers—all of which he had encouraged—were summarily dismissed. His pride could engulf the room in flames. And if you asked him why he had no experienced people, nobody in their forties or fifties or sixties or seventies working alongside him, authoritative people who might contradict him, he would argue that those people had already been corrupted. I was often the only person over thirty-five near him, apart from himself, of course, and he didn't see the problem. He didn't see the cult-leader aspect.

But there was trouble brewing at the house. It first emerged when he told me that they might move to Jemima Khan's house in Oxfordshire. He said the situation at Vaughan's was becoming untenable. Vaughan's "body language" was terrible and he was clearly turning against them, Julian said. A lot of it appeared to be to do with how much Vaughan was charging him to be there. Julian also said that Vaughan was busy with a documentary that he was supposed to have been making for WikiLeaks. "The footage is mine," said Julian, "and he has now got it into his head that it's his. He's still got all sorts of self-value issues to do with not being credited by the BBC when he was a cameraman in Afghanistan, even when he got shot, and it's all coming out with this."

Harry Stopes, my research assistant, pointed out to me how weird it was that Julian kept going on about Vaughan's obsession with lost credits when he, Julian, was also obsessed with credits and was willing to fight an almost continuous war over them. The hardest fact, however, was that the Smiths had been incredibly kind to Julian. They stood bail for him and gave up their house—Julian said this was mainly to gain publicity for the Frontline Club.

I interviewed Julian in stolen hours in the middle of the night, in the backs of cars, and at my house in Bungay, while Harry gathered childhood material, but we knew we were up against it. Canongate was keen to publish before the summer and had no idea, despite my warnings, how unwilling Julian was. Caroline, his agent, believed he still wanted to produce the book but I knew he didn't: I'd seen the lengths to which he would go to get on another topic and knew he'd rather spend hours googling himself than have his own say in the pages of his autobiography. I'd come into this fascinated by the "self" aspect of it all, but the person whose name would be on the cover had both too much self and not enough. Still, we staggered on.

I wrote through the night to assemble what we had. The thinness could become a kind of statement, I asserted; it could become a modernist autobiography. But the jokes wouldn't hold and Julian, despite promising his publishers and me that he'd produce pages, paragraphs, even notes toward his book, produced nothing in the months I was there. Not a single written sentence came from him in all that time. But at the end, from all those exhausting late-night interviews, we assembled a rough draft of 70,000 words. It wasn't by any means great, but it had a voice, a reasonable, even-tempered, slightly amused but moral voice, which was as invented as anything I'd ever produced in fiction.

Yet it hadn't felt like creating a character in a novel so much as writing a voice-over for a real person who wasn't quite real. His vanity and the organization's need for money couldn't resist the project, but he never really considered the outcome, that I'd be there, making marks on a page that would in some way represent what he said about his experiences and his ideas. The issue of control never became real to Julian. He should have felt worried about what he was supplying, but he never did—he had in this, as in everything, a broad illusion of control. Only once did he turn to me and show a glint of understanding. "People think you're helping me write my book," he said, "but actually I'm helping you write your novel."

The publishers were keen to have a draft of the book ready by March 31 and he took that even less seriously. But I had to take it seriously—we had a contract. I closed the first draft on time and we sat, Harry Stopes and I, in Bungay with the laptop hot and a heap of manuscript marked with indications of where new chapters might come. That night Harry spell-checked it and added stuff and we took it over to Ellingham Hall on a memory stick. This was intended to be the copy that Julian would add to, subtract from, and approve. When we arrived, the kitchen was full of WikiLeaks staff, all gathered excitedly around a laptop. They were drinking mojitos and Skyping with an Australian producer who wanted to make a cable show about WikiLeaks's "adventures" around the world. That day, Julian had become hot under the collar about the idea of the draft being shown to the editors in London. (Harry was due to deliver the draft to Canongate the next day.) The American editor, Dan Frank of Knopf, had flown over for the purpose, and the Canongate editor, Nick Davies, was waiting with him in London. You have to remember this was all very close to the intended date of publication.

"They shouldn't be allowed to read it at all," Julian suddenly said, while the mojito party went on around him.

"They're the editors," I said. "They've commissioned this thing. And they have to read it."

"No. They will only prejudice it."

"That's their prerogative."

"No. Give me the phone."

Julian then called Nick at Canongate and stood up to walk into the hall. "This is not an editorial event," he said. "As a favor, we'll let you read the manuscript in its present form." He then proceeded to tell Nick that Harry would invigilate during the reading, and would destroy the copies when the reading was over. I told Julian this was a terrible idea. Harry was mortified and said so immediately. But Julian insisted. I appealed to Sarah, saying this was the sort of high-handed stuff that turned allies into enemies. She said nothing. I decided to wait until I heard from Jamie Byng. Julian's previous suggestion, by the way, was that the editors come to Norfolk and read it in front of him. I nixed that as being a complete insult, and so he came up with the idea that Harry should invigilate. Jamie duly texted me: "Is he suggesting that Dan, Nick, me and Harry all read in the same room? Madness. Nick will ensure the manuscripts are shredded. But at this rate I'm thinking we probably just tell Julian a white lie. Or to stop being ridiculous!"

As we were getting set to leave Ellingham, Julian came up to me beside the Aga and hugged me. "Thanks," he said. We were still talking about possible titles. Earlier on, I had come up with *Disclosure*, but he said he didn't like one-word titles. He preferred *Ban This Book*. (I told him it was too like Abbie Hoffman's *Steal This Book*.) He also liked, bizarrely, *Wet Cement*. (Don't ask.) I countered with *My Life in Secrets*. And Harry felt it could be called *Assange by Assange*, before admitting this sounded too much like a perfume. The gang was communally molesting a computer, the producer had gone out into the Australian sunshine to have a smoke, and the people around the laptop were booing, jealous of the good weather. Julian came to the door with a drink in his hand and waved us into the dark. "Andy," he cried as I made for the car. "Don't let them push you around." He was talking about his publishers, who had collectively paid $2.5 million for his autobiography.

Jamie's white lie had taken effect, and all the editors took custody of the manuscript on Friday. They began reading immediately and the texts came soon afterward. Nick said he and Dan were thrilled and it was just what they'd hoped for. Jamie was excited and I just felt relieved that we hadn't opened with a disaster. I knew that Julian would have much to alter, and would introduce untold delays—they were now hoping for June—but the book contained the basic material culled from those dozens of hours of infuriating interviews and the thing had moved forward.

Julian had promised to read the draft over the weekend and the British publishers were coming to see him on Monday morning. I'd agreed to have the meeting at my house in Bungay because Julian was too easily distracted at Ellingham Hall. Jamie and Nick from Canongate arrived early. Julian and Sarah were due at 9:30 a.m. but turned up an hour late. There was endless tea. Julian eventually sat at the table and turned to Jamie. "How was Friday?" Julian asked.

"Friday was good. The weekend was good . . ."

I looked at Jamie. "He means the reading," I said.

"Oh yeah," Jamie said. "I'm amazed at what's been achieved. It's really good and . . . what did you think?"

Julian fixed him with a fuck-you stare. "I've read about a third of it and it's clear to me it needs a lot of work and won't be ready for June."

There were other statements, preliminary remarks about schedules and timetables, while the realization sank in that Julian hadn't bothered to read the manuscript. "You haven't read it?" Jamie said. "We all agreed to read it over the weekend. You had three whole days to read it. It takes eight hours."

"I had some dangerous things happening around the world," Julian said. "Matters of life and death I had to take care of. These things have to be prioritized."

"That's fine," I said, "but we can't have a discussion about a book you haven't read."

"Well, I've read enough to know that it needs a lot of work and this June date is impossible."

At a guess, I'd say he had read the first three pages. He'd never wanted June as a publication date and the whole project gave him the willies. That hunch was confirmed by everything he said and everything he didn't say. Jamie suddenly became furious. "I'm disappointed. I'm dismayed. Andy worked his arse off to get this manuscript ready and we all traveled up here to discuss it—all having read it over the weekend—and you haven't even bothered to read it."

"I appreciate all the work Andy is doing," Julian said, "but I can't rush into print with something so important. There are legal issues to do with this and my enemies are poised . . ."

I was neither hurt nor surprised. Julian's default position is to assert himself under fire. He had signed up for a book he didn't really want to publish because—as he alleged to me a few weeks earlier—Mark Stephens had suggested it might help cover costs. Now he was forced to take the book seriously for the first time. At some level, it was a kind of ethical disaster for him. He had jogged along with the project and even got to enjoy the process— he loved having an audience, a pupil, an analyst, and, at times, a father—but now the thing had become real and he was totally shocked. Jamie asked him point-blank if he wanted the book to happen.

"I do want it to happen," Julian said, "but on my terms. I never agreed to this June publication date."

Under pressure, Julian agreed that we would sit down with the book from Monday, April 11. He said he would have read it through twice by then, once to get the style of it and a second time to make amendments. He said he would clear whatever time was necessary.

The following Monday was High Noon at the breakfast table in Bungay. Julian was back to his old self, castigating his publishers, but singing at a higher pitch now, saying the art of autobiography was hateful. Men who reveal their private lives in books are "weak," he said. People who write about their family are "prostitutes." And so it went on for hour after excellent hour. "I really like the writing and everything," he said, "but it's too apologetic. There are too many qualifiers." And again: "I can see something you can't see, which is that my opponents will use this material to undermine me. They will dive on this stuff to say I'm weak."

"No, they won't," I said. "They'll see that you know yourself. You can't write an autobiography that merely attempts to second-guess your opponents."

I felt quite sorry for Julian. And I continued to feel sorry for him. He was in a horrible predicament. He had signed up for a project that his basic psychology would not allow. In the smart and admirable way of emotional defense, he dressed his objections in rhetoric and principles, but the reality was much sadder, and much more alarming for him. He didn't know who to be. His remarks, as always, were ostentatiously conceived and recklessly stated. He didn't know what to believe. "These books are used by your enemies to show you in a certain light," he said. "I would never say my stepfather was an alcoholic . . ."

"But you did say it, Julian. All of the material in these chapters is suggested by what you actually said. You said it to me in dozens of interviews over many late nights. I have them all on tape."

"I was tired."

"But you weren't tired when you allowed them to be transcribed. You weren't tired when you sought an agent to make this deal and signed the contracts. You spoke personally throughout, and never once suggested you didn't want that material used."

"I didn't manage things properly."

"No, you've changed your mind. That's fine. Not fine, but that's the way it is. But you can't say you were tired."

"I was tired. And I was busy."

"Julian. You signed on to write an autobiography and you chose a writer to help you do it. You might consider what you are doing by now saying you didn't want the material you gave to be used in a narrative."

"But private writing is cheap."

"So be it. Don't publish it."

"All these books where men spill their guts and write about their intimate lives . . ."

"That's the story you told. You spoke these words freely into a recorder. You spoke about Brett's drink problem. You spoke endlessly about the cult leader who followed you and your mother . . ."

"But I didn't want it in the book."

"Okay. Then it should be removed."

I could have raised several flags on top of each of his sentences. They showed he was at home. But at home to Julian means he is fully inhabiting his paranoia and fully suspicious about people and things he thinks are out to get him. In some fundamental way he could never have someone write an e-mail for him, let alone a book. As somebody once wrote of somebody else, he is the sort of person who is always swimming toward the life raft. I threw him a line. "What do you want from this book?"

"Facts. Some feelings. But it should be a manifesto. It can have some reflections from childhood and whatever, but the book should be a manifesto of my ideas. It should be like moral essays. And it should have like a plot. Not with personal stuff but a sense of transition."

"And what is this plot of your life that you'd like to relate?"

"I'm not at all interested in a book that is personal. I've always known this."

"So now you're talking about a book of ideas?"

He just stared at me, as if he were a child who had lost his homework and I were an admonishing teacher.

"Need more manifesto."

"Okay," I said. "But *you* have to write that. A manifesto comes from belief. It can't be second-guessed or ghostwritten."

"I agree. I'm going to sit down and do that. I want to get my ideas about justice and power into it. It's like those writings political leaders often did in prison."

"That's fine. It's your book. But you have to tell the publishers very clearly that what you're writing is not an autobiography."

"It's got some personal elements."

"But you've railed against autobiography. You must make it clear to them or they won't accept it. Jamie and his colleagues have been selling this around the world on the understanding that it's your life story. You've allowed them to do that and you've allowed me to write that based on my interviews with you these last two months."

"This will sell even better. And Sonny Mehta seemed much more excited by the idea of a manifesto than some standard autobiography."

"Okay. Make it clear to them."

"The book I'm describing is the book I've always said I would write."

"It wasn't the book you were writing when you stayed up with me all night telling me your stepfather was an alcoholic."

"That's not going in the book. None of that was meant for the book and that's why it was a mistake ever to let them see this early draft, because it has contaminated their minds."

Even if you were the most radical dude on campus, there was always some tight hippie ready to tell you that you were bourgeois for liking, say, Earl Grey tea or for reading Anthony Powell. In that same vein, Julian scorns all attempts at social graces. He eats like a pig. He marches through doors and leaves women in his wake. He talks over everybody. And all his life he has depended on being the impish one, the eccentric one, the boy with a bag full of Einstein who liked climbing trees. But at forty years old, that's less charming, and I found his egotism at the dinner table to be a form of madness more striking than anything he said.

The next day when Julian turned up at the house in Bungay there was soup. He nodded for some and Harry put it down. Julian continued tapping into his laptop. My head was full of the previous night, when Jamie had called after midnight to discuss the problem. "We've sold this book to forty publishers around the world on the basis that it's his autobiography," he said, "and if this motherfucker wants now to denounce that kind of book we'll cancel the contract. I have such a strong feeling for what they've done as an organization, but if he does this he will hurt Canongate and all the others. It's unbelievable." Jamie kept coming back to the "irresponsibility" of someone signing a contract and taking large sums to write a book they couldn't countenance. "We love this early draft and it has the makings of a bestseller that will rescue his reputation. What is he thinking? I'm going down to see Sonny right now."

In the morning, Jamie had sent me a copy of the contract between Canongate and Knopf and Julian. It contained an addendum, written by Sonny, just before it was signed, that detailed what the book must include. It was all the standard autobiography stuff plus a paragraph about his ideas. The clear expectation was that he would deliver a life story with childhood, parents, the hacking years, the trial, and the setting up of WikiLeaks.

This was all in my head as we sat down at the table in Bungay, me, him, Sarah, and Harry the researcher. After a few minutes of Julian tapping on his laptop, I asked him if he'd heard anything from Caroline Michel, his agent. "They're all panicking," he said. "They're such schoolgirls."

"Jamie sent me the contract," I said. "It's clearly different from what you were discussing yesterday."

Julian said, "Have we got it?" Sarah produced a copy on her laptop. He looked at it and immediately focused on the one clause that mentioned his philosophy and said: "See, it's there."

Sarah: "No. Look at the first few clauses. That's what Andy's talking about."

Julian: "See, there it is. My philosophy."

Me: "You're homing in on the bit that suits you. The rest of the addendum stipulates your life story."

Julian: "I don't see what the problem is. Something like that can be interpreted as the book I'm writing. We can give them any book and they'll like it: the food will cause the appetite."

Sarah: "You're now saying a manifesto, a very different sort of book from what they're suggesting here."

Julian (shouting): "I'm fucking never talking to anybody again. They take what they want to hear and twist it through their own paranoia to only hear what fits."

I looked at Harry. "Julian, you said that Sonny would be happy with a manifesto but it's clear what he expects."

Julian: "They need to stop interfering with the soup while it's being cooked. Who's actually read it?"

Me: "Jamie Byng, Nick Davies, Dan from Knopf, and Sonny Mehta."

Julian: "I thought it was just the two editors?"

Me: "No. Jamie was always going to read it. And then they must have given it to Sonny."

Julian looked at Harry. "I thought you were invigilating. You were supposed to take the manuscript away."

"At the end of the day," Harry said, "I'm employed by Canongate. I couldn't refuse when they wanted to keep it. They're my employers."

Julian: "I gave you strict instructions not to let them boss you around. You should have taken it and walked out."

Harry: "They're my employers. I couldn't do that."

Me: "You can't expect him to go against them. This is ludicrous."

Julian: "I'm unspeakably angry. I didn't know your loyalty was to them . . . a publisher's spy in the drafting process."

Harry: "Do you mean me?"

Julian: "Yes." At which point he went into the garden slamming the door behind him.

Harry: "What a prat."

Julian stood in the garden and stared over the fields. In the past, Sarah had covered for him when he was out of order, but now she didn't. She just apologized and said it was crazy. After a few minutes, Julian came back and picked up his things, saying nothing. Eventually: "Sarah, pack up." He left the house and they drove away. About ten minutes later I got a text from him saying he wasn't angry with me and was sorry not to have said goodbye. Harry asked if he'd done anything wrong. Of course he hadn't. He didn't even remember calling Julian a prat.

Caroline Michel was due to arrive the day after for an 11:00 a.m. meeting at Ellingham Hall. Julian called me and asked if I'd sit in. "That's fine," I said, though I felt it was yet another irregularity. He came and picked me up on the way for his signing-in at Beccles police station. In the car, he railed against his lawyers, alleging Mark Stephens had brought in his own team. He asked me how a writer normally gets an agent. "Well, you go and see a few of them. Then you make a decision about which one's best for you."

"See. That's what I mean. I didn't see anyone. Mark Stephens brought in Caroline and now I've got this whole situation . . . Everyone's making money out of this."

Back at the house, Sarah was more depressed than I'd ever seen her. She implied that last night had been difficult and she'd had to take some of the blame for seeming to agree with us in the dispute over who got to read the manuscript. Julian's habit was to turn these young staff members on and off like a tap: he knew they were devoted to him and he took pains to outmaneuver them, even when there was no real need. She sat very sullen on the sofa in the drawing room and barely looked up.

"What's wrong with Sarah?" Caroline whispered when she arrived from the station.

"A bit depressed," I said. We went into the kitchen and I stood with my back to the Aga.

"The first thing I have to say is this is a brilliant read," she said. "So exciting. Gosh. Just fabulous."

"Please don't say that," Julian said. "If you say that to the publishers they'll just want to publish it." Caroline looked at me as if she had taken a wrong turn into the Twilight Zone. "How did you get the manuscript anyhow?" he asked.

"Sonny gave me his copy."

Julian immediately went white and began to shake with rage. "See! That's what I fucking mean," he said. "Passing 'round the manuscript! No one except those two editors was supposed to see it and I'm just fucking furious."

"Don't be furious," said Caroline. "It doesn't matter . . ."

"It does matter! Manuscripts flying across the Atlantic!"

"Julian, come on," I said. "You can't complain about your *agent* reading it."

"I don't mind her reading it, but WHO ELSE is reading it?"

Caroline had tactfully started calling the "manifesto" stuff the "vision part," which was likely to appeal more to the publishers. But whenever she spoke of what she liked about the autobiographical material in the draft, he shut her down. She plunged on, trying to sew the various bits of opposition into a seamless pattern, but there was a lot of optimism in what she said. He said he thought the book could come out in 2012. "How about July for delivery?" she said.

"Impossible."

"But let's try." He said more about how he'd like the book to be and she brought out the part of the contract written by Sonny. She said what he was saying met the requirements of the contract. It didn't, and I wondered what her strategy was, but I'd said as much as I wanted to say. Eventually, Julian agreed to two things. He would mark up the draft, showing what was publishable, by his lights, and striking out what wasn't. And then he would sit down and write the "vision bit." He said he would start right away and in three or four weeks, if we left him alone, he would have it.

I spent most of the next few weeks in Scotland on family business. Julian sent me a message while I was in the Highlands saying "Big up, Mr O'Hagan," a reference he knew I would get, to what a convict had written to him in prison: "Big up, Mr WikiLeaks." Other than that, and a few hellos through Sarah, we hadn't spoken since the day he agreed to start writing.

I rang Caroline on May 9 and repeated that the book could be completed but Julian had to want it to happen. Then Jamie rang. He said Julian hadn't done much at all and was on "radio

silence." Jamie, as often on this project, went from being conciliatory to being outraged, and again began to talk about canceling the contract. "He's in breach," Jamie said, "and if the book is
pushed beyond September the publishers around the world will
begin canceling."

Julian was getting a lot of flak in the press for making
WikiLeaks employees sign contracts threatening them with a
£12 million lawsuit if they disclosed anything about the organization. It was clear he didn't see the problem. He has a notion that
WikiLeaks floats above other organizations and their rules. He
can't understand why any public body should keep a secret but
insists that his own organization enforce its secrecy with lawsuits.
Every time he mentioned legal action against *The Guardian* or *The
New York Times*, and he did this a lot, I would roll my eyes, but
he didn't see the contradiction. He was increasingly lodged in a
jungle of his own making, and I told Jamie it was like trying to
write a book with Mr. Kurtz.

Caroline and I made another visit to Norfolk. When we arrived, Julian hugged us both. "Hello, friend," he said to me, in a
rather formal way—clearly he was gesturing toward my father
having died since we last met. The Boateng suit was now grubby
and he seemed imprisoned in it. That morning was the point
where it all went to another level of ghastliness. He had devel-
oped a proper siege mentality. I thought this must have to do
with Vaughan and the bad atmosphere at Ellingham Hall, but it
was more than that: he had grown to feel his lawyers were the
enemy. "It's disgusting," he said, when we sat down with Caroline in the drawing room. "I'm not doing any more work on the
book until it's guaranteed that the money is not going to the
lawyers."

"Well, it goes where you want it to go."

"Disgusting . . ."

"Nobody pays their full lawyers' bill," Caroline said.

"I'm not paying it. They've charged me for sitting on a fucking train. I should never have stayed in this country in the first place: I should have flown this jurisdiction."

"Yes, well, let's . . . There's a lot of pressure coming from the publishers."

"I'm on strike. I would rather hack my leg off than let someone fuck me. Do you know how much the whole Max Mosley case cost?" He was talking about big legal cases. "Four hundred thousand pounds. Do you know how much *Tesco v. The Guardian* cost? Four hundred thousand pounds."

Caroline: "How much do you think they should be paid?"

Julian named a figure.

Caroline: "I think it's going to have to be a bit more than that."

A week later Julian called to say there "might be time" to look at the book. The question of time was always bizarre. He said he couldn't meet these impossible deadlines, but while the ship was going down, he didn't miss a single interview, festival, or award ceremony, and he gave fancy reasons for that, about feeding his public.

After snow and what seemed like months of rain, the garden at Ellingham Hall was now in full bloom. Nobody was up when I arrived except Vaughan Smith, who opened the door and chatted to me in the kitchen. Vaughan wasn't aware I knew anything about the tension between him and Julian, and he understandably fished for detail about how it was all going. I didn't tell him much, though it must have been obvious to him how chaotic things were. He was critical of the people around Julian and said that nearly everyone who came into contact with him was looking to make something. Whether he knew it or not, Smith himself was constantly accused of this, mainly by Julian.

Julian came downstairs laughing and asked me to come with him to the police station. We jumped into the car with Sarah driving and he started excitedly telling me about some people he'd got in Afghanistan who were trying to find out about bias in the Afghan media. It emerged, over a few telephone calls in the car, that the guys in Afghanistan had no contacts and were stuck for something to do, so Julian called Kristinn Hrafnsson, his Icelandic colleague, who tried to drum something up. I later heard Julian call a contact at an activist group to find some people on the ground who might direct his people to a story. It was impressive to see him, on the way to the police station, doing the work of a journalist, and he was good at it. When he wants, he can deploy a kind of ethical charm that gets things done. The contact gave him some numbers and he passed them on to his crew. I say "crew," because I believe they were the ones doing the cable TV show based on WikiLeaks' work around the world. Along with legal arguments and his fights with various media groups, this was his major preoccupation for months. In the car, we also discussed Alex Gibney, the Oscar-winning documentary filmmaker who was slated to do a film on Julian (the film, *We Steal Secrets*, came out in 2013). "There's a problem of editorial input," Julian said. "We want to have some control. But the guy is, like, quite underhanded. He has that arrogance. Then he sent a colleague to talk to us and we're so used to people recording me that we had her frisked for recording devices, and he sent this furious message about what a terrible insult, et cetera." Julian was always very interested in the movie arrangements being cooked up. "Movie rights" on the book were uppermost in his mind. He talked about them a lot, though he also spoke critically of the filmmakers who had expressed interest in him. He was happy to dismiss Paul Greengrass, Alex Gibney, or Steven Spielberg with a flick of the tongue.

The three of us went to a very pink café in the town and ordered sandwiches and cakes. We sat outside, and Julian got distracted by some young girls walking past. "Hold on," he said, and turned his gaze. "No," he said. "It was fine until I saw the teeth." One of the girls was wearing braces. When Sarah came back and asked what we were talking about, Julian said he'd been admiring some fourteen-year-old girls, "until they came close." I record this not to show how predatory Julian is—I don't believe he is any more predatory than hundreds of men I've known. It's not that: I tell it to suggest how self-delighted he can be. He doesn't at all see how often his self-delight leads him into trouble. He doesn't understand other people in the slightest and it would be hard to think of a leader who so reliably gets everyone wrong, mistaking people's motivations, their needs, their values, their gifts, their loyalty, and thereby destroying their usefulness to him. He was always very solicitous with me when I was with him, but I could tell he responded much more to the fact that I like a joke than to the notion that I was a professional writer. The latter mattered to him for five seconds when he was trying to find a writer to work with, but it was the time-wasting, authority-baiting side that really kept our relationship alive. He thought I was his creature and he forgot what a writer is: someone with a tendency to write things down and perhaps seek the truth and aim for transparency.

He was in a state of panic at all times that things might get out. But he manages people so poorly, and is such a slave to what he's not good at, that he forgets he might be making bombs set to explode in his own face. I am sure this is what happens in many of his scrapes: he runs on a high-octane belief in his own rectitude and wisdom, only to find later that other people had their own views—of what is sound journalism or agreeable sex—and the idea that he might be complicit in his own mess baffles him. Fact is, he was not in control of himself and most of what his former colleagues said about him just might be true. He is thin-skinned, conspiratorial, untruthful, narcissistic, and he thinks he owns the material he conduits. It may turn out that Julian is not Daniel Ellsberg or John Wilkes, but Charles Foster Kane, abusive and monstrous in his pursuit of the truth that interests him, and a man who, it turns out, was motivated all the while not by high principles but by a deep sentimental wound. Perhaps we won't know until the final frames of the movie.

Sitting outside the café, he was mulling over some more re-cent wounds. "I suppose it would look right, to show leniency. He should be told I am making a gesture of generosity." He was talking about Harry Stopes.

"Whatever," I said. "He's a research assistant and this should be forgotten about."

"He shouldn't have called me a prat behind my back."

"He didn't do it behind your back. He said it to your face, but you were busy slamming the door at the time."

"Well . . ."

"The much more important thing is how we get this book done. I've got to move on soon. I was only supposed to be helping you until the first of April. The trouble is you're just not focused on this book."

"I am. It just needs to be done in a certain way. There's a big fan base out there. They will buy this book if it contains the right message and inspires them."

"What do we need?"

"It needs to be more like Ayn Rand."

I was stunned for a second. This was new. "I don't know if

I can help you with that," I said. He took out his phone and made another call about Afghanistan.

Back at Ellingham Hall the sun had chased all the gloom out of the dining room. I looked at the table next to the window and remembered laying all the chapter cards there back in January and trying to visualize a shape for the book. I hardly knew Julian then, but he looked over the layout and agreed to it, and I remember thinking this might be a good collaboration. At first, as we inspected those cards in the middle of the night, I thought he saw an opportunity laid out before him, to tell it like it was, to step out of all the bluster and tell the truth. But now, on this bright morning, I saw he liked fame more. He was talking to Sarah and me about his forthcoming trip to the Hay Festival. "You've been there, right?" he said.

It seemed mad to me that he was considering going to a book festival to talk about a book that wasn't done, wasn't published, and might never be published.

"I'll read one of those good writing parts of yours," he said. "And then I'll read a new political thing. The latter will get the headlines and the first will surprise people." I was astonished. *The Daily Telegraph* was sending a helicopter to take him down to Hay. He wanted me to come with him.

"I hate helicopters," I said. "I'm not coming to Hay to talk about a book that isn't written. Even less, to talk about a book I was supposed to be helping you write in secret. Why would I do that?"

"It might be good for fly on the wall," he said. "I'd like more fly on the wall in the book."

He kept saying he'd done some work on the early draft but

he couldn't find it. That afternoon, as I laid out a second-draft plan for the book, Julian searched the laptops in the room—about eight of them—for his "marked-up" version. There was something pathetic about the search: it was clear he had never marked up any version.

He couldn't really bear to think about it. He was relentlessly autobiographical in his speech, but he clearly felt trapped by the requirement to commit to a narrative that would become the "story." The business of the marked-up text seemed to be decisive and I felt we were fucked. By now, he had found at least half a dozen major obstacles. When it wasn't deadlines, it was his view that all autobiography is "prostitution"; when it wasn't that, it was not having the time to read the material or being too tired to do the interviews, or needing six weeks on his own just to sit down and "focus" on his vision, or hating the idea of all the money going to his lawyers. I've never been with anybody who made me feel so like an adult. And I say that as the father of a thirteen-year-old.

We agreed I'd come back in a few days and all his marking up would be done. "I'm going to look for this for a while longer and then give up," said Julian, still examining laptops. At the same time, Tristan, one of his random young assistants, who was studying video production at Bournemouth, was looking through film footage that we might use for "scenes" in the book. He gave me a hard drive to take away. When I got it home, I saw the main piece of footage (there are three hundred hours more) was of Julian having a shave as everyone watched.

Under his bail conditions, Julian could make trips in the daytime so long as he was back at Ellingham Hall by 10:00 p.m. It was my birthday and I was having dinner with friends in the St. Pancras Hotel when Julian rang to say he wanted to come to London. He arrived at my place the next day with two of his colleagues, a nice albino bloke whom I'd never met and a shy American girl. As soon as he came into the flat, Julian went off checking for bugs, he said, or exits, or the sleepover situation— these appear to be his priorities wherever he goes. I took him into the sitting room and he slumped on the sofa. He looked absolutely shattered, his clothes were done in, and he seemed hunted. I asked if he was hungry and got him a slice of cake.

By now he was referring to his lawyers as "cunts." He told me Stephens accused him of hanging his arse out to dry by asking for the bill to be cut. "He's made little cuts—twenty thousand pounds here, forty thousand there, but the bill remains disgusting," Julian said. In an hour's time he was due to go to Camden Town for a meeting with Gareth Peirce, a human rights lawyer, who he hoped would take on the job of representing him at the next appeal hearing.

He hadn't found the marked manuscript and hadn't done any of the things we'd agreed on. We'd lost another four days, and I'd tried to help him further by writing the thing he wouldn't write. I handed him a draft of the "personal vision" stuff and he said he would read it that evening. "No, you won't," I said. "This book isn't going to happen, is it?" He looked at me with a degree of honesty, I felt, for the first time. "You haven't put pen to paper once in all these months. You find the whole thing difficult and you can't face it. You now have to tell the publishers straight, you can't do it."

"I know."

"You've got to lead this thing. There's over two million dollars and more than forty secondary publishers. You can't keep mucking everybody about and thinking it's going to be okay. Just stop the train now."

"The book will happen, but later . . ."

"I know. But your contract is for now. And your contract is for an autobiography. Pay Canongate back the money you've taken from them. It's important you pay them back. The others . . ."

"Can sue me."

"Whatever you say. But nobody died. Just pay back the money and maybe you'll have a book to write in a few years further down the line. There's a reason many people don't publish their memoirs until the end of their careers."

"Let's leave it for a week," he said. "I'll know my legal position better soon."

"Have a present," he said at the door. He gave me a tin of General White Portion, a kind of snuff. "From Sweden," he said with a smile. I shook my head and closed the door.

"You're the person holding this together," Jamie said when I eventually spoke to him. But I wasn't happy to be that person. I didn't sign up to be the executive producer. Then news came that the Icelandic publishers wanted to cancel their contract. Other foreign publishers were getting cold feet. Jamie wrote a letter to Julian and Caroline Michel and sent me a copy, with a covering note. "If this doesn't wake Julian from his slumber," he said, "then I fear it is Game Over."

Julian phoned to ask if I'd reconsider and come on the helicopter to Hay the next day. I said I was looking after my daughter. He said to bring her, too. "No," I said. With Julian, in every case, spectacle overrules tactics, and he couldn't see that me stepping out of a helicopter at Hay with him was not a good idea. He also told me he had signed on the dotted line with Gareth Peirce.

Sarah called to say she wanted to meet me and give me a hard drive. It was full of secrets and she had to hand it to me personally. She was having lunch with a friend in London and we arranged for her to come to my place in the afternoon. She arrived about 3:00. I made coffee and she sat at the kitchen table and unloaded about the organization and Julian for two hours. "He's, like, threatened to fire me a few times," she said, "and always for crazy reasons. One of the times was literally because I had hugged another member of staff. Hugged him, like a friend hug. Julian was like 'That's so disrespectful to me' and went off on one. He said I'd said the guy smelled nice and that was humiliating. He did smell nice; he'd just had a bath. Julian was furious. And once he was like 'You're the new Domscheit-Berg' and 'You could do some damage if you left.' He won't tell the others what my role is, so one time he's like 'You're my number two' but he won't say to the others. So, if I try to speak to Kristinn he's like 'Who do you think you are?' because I've got no, like, official authority. Only Julian has that."

She told me there had been a big bust-up over a deal in Canada because Julian, having negotiated with the CBC and some Canadian press, was about to double-cross them at the last minute and she'd spoken up. He wouldn't just overrule her: he had to spend hours convincing her he was right. "It happens all the time," she said. "He won't do anything and I'll keep reminding him, and then, like with the Canadian elections, he'll jump into action at the very last minute. And he was about to make a massive mistake and I told him. Afterwards, he blamed me for the whole thing and said he'd come close to firing me over that but he probably wouldn't."

We turned to talking about the book. "In fairness," she said, "he never wanted to do it. Mark Stephens was going on about a book and before you knew it Caroline Michel was involved and it was all this money and the thing was signed. He didn't want to write a book but now he's just letting it get worse and worse. He goes on the phone to Jamie to say stuff and then doesn't say it."

"That's a disaster," I said.

"I know," she said. "He doesn't want people to see how his mind works."

I implied that it was weird for someone who liked the sound of their own voice to ask for a ghostwriter. As the conversation went on you could see she was strung between loving him and being baffled. She said she knew that he was only loyal to her because they were "stuck in that house." As soon as he was free he would chase other girls. "He openly chats girls up and has his hand on their arse," she said, "and goes nuts if I even talk to another guy." She said he couldn't stand her being away from him and didn't think she should see friends or go on holiday or "abandon" him at all.

I asked about the rape allegations. I said that in all my time with him he hadn't really clarified what happened. "It was weird," she said. "Like, why was he even staying with those girls? He didn't rape them but he was really fucking stupid."

She said she now understood that people like Domscheit-Berg had a basic point. "I don't agree with the way he did it," she said, "but you can tell he was probably just trying to say something true and got hated for it. That's the way it is with Julian: he can't listen. He doesn't get it. He'll try to get me to ring John Pilger at three in the morning. Some of these sureties gave fifty grand, basically because they were friends of Jemima's, and he thinks he can get them to do stuff for him in the middle of the night. It's crazy."

She said Julian had told her to try to persuade me to come to Hay tomorrow. I said I couldn't. I had my daughter. I said I thought the whole trip was mad. Jamie thought he was going to read from the book and promote it in advance. In fact, he was just going to be interviewed and do the celebrity bit. All the discussions, all the threats, all the attempts at persuasion, and all my work had come to nothing. Julian had known all along he would scupper the book. He just didn't have the balls to tell us all he couldn't do it.

"I don't think he's got the right kind of psychology to be able to put his name to a memoir," I said.

"I know," she said. "But he might want it to become like a fly-on-the-wall record of him."

That's what this is, but he'll hate this, too. The impulse toward free speech, like Sarah speaking freely in my kitchen or me speaking freely now, is permissible only if it adheres to his message. His pursuit of governments and corporations was a ghostly reverse of his own fears for himself. That was the big secret with him: he wanted to cover up everything about himself except his fame.

Reports reached me from Hay. Reactions to his appearance were mixed. He was described as looking puffy and unkempt. Ralph Fiennes, who was in the audience, described the event as "compelling" but suggested it also made him feel deeply uncomfortable.

On June 5, I picked Julian up at Ellingham Hall and drove him to the police station. He got into the car with the print of bedsheets still on his face and his hair sticking up. "Life is so unjust," he said. "I was dreaming I was walking down this very long, steep, rickety path on a beach, many thousands of meters going down into the ocean. I got to a point where there were abandoned pieces of wetsuit, especially feet, and I was in bare feet and really wanted to go into the sea below. I went through the wetsuits and there were some Russian ones and some French ones that must have belonged to crab fishermen. I found one and was just pulling it on—I could see down into the water, and then this terrible alarm clock, Sarah, woke me up."

We called in at a breakfast place in Beccles. He said we should cancel the contract. He said he didn't care what effect this decision would have on the Americans or on his agent, but he did feel bad for Jamie Byng and Canongate. I said again that he must make sure he paid Canongate back. He said that would happen and that his agents held the money. "You and I can keep working together," he said.

"That's fine," I said, "but this contract has either to be honored or canceled. There's no middle way."

"I know," he said. "And it will be canceled. I regret it because I think it would be good to preempt the Swedish case. There's going to be a lot of shit about me in the press there during the trial and they're waiting to give their version, and I should get the truth out there before then."

He asked me to work for him as a kind of "official historian," "coming in and out of the various countries and projects." He said he thought there was a masterpiece of narrative nonfiction lying in wait. "You get to that over time," he said.

"Not in a handful of months."

"Correct."

At that point, Sarah wrote to Caroline Michel that the contract should be canceled. Jamie tried to persuade me to write Julian's authorized biography, offering me half the royalties in advance (about one and a half million dollars), but I refused. Jamie had written to Sonny Mehta hoping the "rescue" book could still be done. But, on the other line, as it were, Julian was telling me there would never be a second book.

A meeting at Ellingham Hall attended by Sonny and others was excruciating. Sonny had to sit for two hours while Julian lectured him about power, corruption, the police state, and the truth about publishing. The editor in chief of Knopf said almost nothing.

The charade of Julian Assange writing a book finally came to an end at one o'clock at Cigala in Lamb's Conduit Street. It was 159 days after Jamie had arrived at my flat to lay out the plan, and he came into the restaurant the same guy, not much defeated, and ready to go for another twelve rounds. During that time, Egypt and Tunisia had won a questionable freedom, Libya had gone to war, I'd toured Australia, my father had died, I'd given up smoking, and I'd managed to say nothing about the fact that Julian Assange had asked me to help him find his voice and then asked me to help him unfind it. It was a good season to be a listener and a bad one to be a talker, so I'd followed that ethos to the letter.

It was Evelyn Waugh who said that when a writer is born into a family the family is over. And why would it be any different when a second family comes to call? Julian wanted a brother, a friend, a PR guru, a chief of staff, a speechwriter, and he wanted that person to be a writer with a reputation. When he was working with those fellows from *The Guardian*, *The New York Times*, and *Der Spiegel*, he allowed himself to forget that they were journalists with decades of experience and their own fund of beliefs. To him they were just conduits and possible disciples: he is still reeling, even today, from the shock that they were their own men and women. My discussions with him would go on, in private, long after the idea of "collaboration" was over. But he consistently forgot that I am foremost a writer and an independent person. Julian is an actor who believes all the other lines in the play are there to feed his lines; that none of the other lives is substantial in itself. People have inferred from this kind of thing that he has Asperger's syndrome, and they could be right. He sees every idea as a mere spark from a fire in his own mind. That way madness lies, of course, and the extent of Julian's lying convinced me that he is probably a little mad, sad, and bad, for all the glory of

WikiLeaks as a project. For me, the clarifying moment in our relationship came when he so desperately wanted me to join him on the helicopter flight to Hay. He wanted me to see him on the helicopter and he wanted me to assist him in living out that version of himself. The fact that he was going to a book festival to talk about a book we both knew he would never produce was immaterial: he was flying in from Neverland with his own personal J. M. Barrie. What could be nicer for the lost boy of Queensland with his silver hair and his sense that the world of adults is no real place for him? By refusing the helicopter I was not refusing that side of him, only allowing myself the distance to see it clearly for what it was. And to see myself clearly, too: I have had to fight to grow away from my own lost boy, and it seemed right that day to fly a kite with my daughter and retain my independence from this man's confused dream of himself.

For the lunch with Jamie at Cigala, I asked that my agent, Derek Johns, come too, and suggested Caroline Michel should also be there. Before Caroline arrived, Jamie said he hoped the book could now become *Assange* by Andrew O'Hagan. He said he'd already begun to persuade Julian that this was not a book he could have a veto on, and that it would be the best chance of getting his message out. "He's never going to be in this position again, with a writer he trusts, a writer who already knows the material. He says he's willing as long as he could help set out what the book should contain."

"He might agree to that now," I said, "but he will make every effort to injunct that book come publication. Believe me. You are setting yourself up for a major nightmare by imagining that this first-person book, which he hates, can just be shunted into the third person and published. It's the same material and he will oppose it."

Derek agreed. Jamie eventually saw that the book would not

happen on those terms. The question of collaboration in that sense was over: even to pay Julian a penny would assume his authorization, and I wouldn't work on another book given how the present attempt had failed. I told Jamie I would continue to follow the activities of the organization in my own time and with no certain end in mind.

"Did Julian ever get those e-mails to you," Caroline asked, "the ones about the setting up of WikiLeaks?"

"No," I said. He never located any material. Just like he never located the marked-up manuscript. "And what would be the point in having them? He doesn't want a book."

"But he does want a book. Every time I speak to him he says: 'I want a book.'"

"And what does that mean, 'I want a book'? He wants a book by not allowing it to be written? By not doing the work? By not committing himself to the interviews or liking what emerges from them? In what sense does he want a book?"

"I don't know."

"He doesn't want a book. And all basis for a collaboration as defined by this contract is over."

"That's right," Jamie said. "You've already explained to him we expect the money paid back in full. And the same for Knopf. And sadly the contracts are canceled."

"He prefers to say 'suspended,'" said Caroline.

"No," said Derek. "You have to be clear. This is not suspended and it is not postponed. It is canceled."

"But he says he wants to continue working with Andy," Caroline said. There was a pause in which she and I exchanged long glances. I think she wanted me to save the day somehow. "It's just so frustrating," she added, "because there's a very good book waiting there."

"I know," I said. "But he can't handle it."

"Mark Stephens thinks he's having a nervous breakdown."

"That's possible, too," I said.

One of the issues that bugged me was how far all this had taken us from the work WikiLeaks had started out doing. I believed at this stage that the organization could regroup after the legal appeals and the autobiography battle, returning to the core work that had made Julian's name. But there was strong evidence now that he was devoted to his legal problems as well as to skirmishes with former collaborators over his reputation. The issue of Bradley (now Chelsea) Manning's court-martial was very much on his mind but he didn't seem able to lead the charge in defending Manning, and for a good reason: it remained important to him to pretend not to know Manning was the source for the Apache helicopter video, the cables, and the Afghan war logs that had justified WikiLeaks's presence as a new moral force in the world. I remained sure that the real research on the cables hadn't been done, that the implications of so much military and diplomatic plotting, though they could change the map, hadn't been looked into. I thought, if Julian was serious and strategic, that WikiLeaks should not only bale stuff out onto the Web but should then facilitate the editing and presenting of that work in a way that was of permanent historical value. Perry Anderson, the historian and proprietor of Verso Books, had the same thought, and I put it to Julian a few weeks after the Cigala lunch that the WikiLeaks Map of the World should be a series that provided for a proper academic study of what the biggest security leaks in history had revealed, with expert commentary, notes, essays, and introductions. It would provide the organization with a lasting, grown-up legacy, a powerful, orderly continuation of its initial work.

Julian came to lunch at my flat in Belsize Park. Tariq Ali

came, too, and so did Mary-Kay Wilmers, the editor of the *London Review of Books*, as well as an American editor for Verso called Tom Mertes. Anderson's idea was that Verso would publish a series of books, or one book in which each chapter showed how the U.S. cables released by WikiLeaks had changed the political position of a particular country. A writer who knew, say, Italy would introduce the chapter and the same would be done for every country, and it would be very meticulous and well-made. Julian gave a big speech at the beginning, the middle, and the end of the lunch. He clearly liked Tariq but had no sense of him as someone who knew a lot more about the world than he did. Although the idea for the book had come from Verso, Julian preferred to give a lecture about how most academics were corrupted by their institutions.

During the lunch I asked Julian if he had done anything about Canongate. He said everything was fine over there. "Not so," I said. "The problem isn't going to go away. You owe them half a million pounds." He wanted a cigar and I found him one. "It'll be fine," he said. Anyone else would have jumped at the chance of the Verso project, but as Julian drove off in a taxi I knew he would never call Tariq about this or lay any of the groundwork they'd agreed on. Julian was already more concerned about claiming the idea for himself, an ambitious idea that he would never see to fruition. The meeting had called for responsible action, when what Julian loved was irresponsible reaction. Half a decade later, a much less ambitious book would appear from Verso, a single volume, good in itself but, for me, a reminder of the copious ill-application that was obvious throughout my time with Assange, and which flowed with the wine and the monologuing at that lunch in Belsize Park.

An invitation arrived for his fortieth birthday. "Come and celebrate with the 'Most Dangerous Man in the World,'" it said.

In London, there had been a touch of the old radical chic when people heard there was to be a party. A film director, a therapist, and a writer left messages on my voice mail asking if I was going to the "big party." When it came to the day I brought a friend full of curiosity and we arrived at Ellingham Hall to find a kind of tent that is popular at your average big fat gypsy wedding. Julian's dad was there, and I spoke to him, not gleaning anything, just capturing the sense of this rather proud and gentle man. The party was curiously unfestive, somehow, like one of those family occasions where nobody has really thought about the music or the fact that the kids will want different things from the adults. There was a lame auction of stuff Julian had in prison, too egotistical, I thought, and, again, a little off-key. Vivienne Westwood was waving her arms around and bidding. Jennifer Robinson, the lawyer who assisted Mark Stephens, and I had a brief chat and she was literally rolling her eyes about what had transpired. "We need to talk," she said. "What's happening? The whole thing is running out of control." From the next table, Jemima Khan crooked her hand in the way that means "call me."

At the end of July 2011, Canongate told me they intended to publish the first draft of the book without Julian's say-so, and with an unsigned foreword by Nick Davies, the editor, outlining the reasons it was being published despite being incomplete and not having Julian's authorization. As far as I was concerned it felt right neither to help them with the book nor to hinder their efforts to get their money back. The dispute was between Julian and the people whose contract he signed.

On August 7, Nick from Canongate came to the flat I was staying at in Glasgow (I had a play in rehearsal) from his office in Edinburgh. He was worried about his foreword and about the manuscript more generally, and I agreed to look at it with a view to protecting each side from warfare. Nick's foreword made every attempt to be decent, stating clearly how Canongate felt the book met their intentions and the letter of the contract, but making clear it was not being published with Julian's authorization. I made several suggestions. I advised him to admit that the book was too personal for Julian, which is what Julian had said to me, so as to preempt suggestions that his objections were political.

I flipped through the manuscript and advised Nick also to remove the names of the *Guardian* journalists David Leigh and Nick Davies. It wasn't at all clear whether Julian was being fair to them and I felt the parties might be litigious. Both Leigh and Davies had sent me e-mails saying they would sue if the book libeled them, and I felt that Jamie, despite being generally gungho, should not land himself in a legal mess. The editor agreed to make these changes. We didn't discuss the Swedish chapter, containing Julian's counterstory of the rape allegations, but I reckoned they might have to come back to it. The case was still pending.

Caroline Michel phoned. She said Jamie would not return her calls. Julian now "wanted to talk," and later he would settle on this unwillingness of Jamie's, ignoring the fact that all the unwillingness had been his for four months. How far was he willing to go to fuck everybody off? The answer came on September 1. Having canvassed his followers on Twitter, Julian decided to dump on the Internet the whole cache of 250,000 U.S. cables supplied to him by Chelsea Manning. He blamed *The Guardian*—a tactic I recognized from many of his sorties—and especially David Leigh. He insisted Leigh had included a password in his book that could decrypt the files WikiLeaks had left online. Leigh has always said this is nonsense. The maneuver brought so many infamous Julian tropes together: the hatred of the United States; the showing off about security while having no real sense of how it works (why were the files left online?); the "blame culture" in which any enemy of his must be shown to have failed. By then, Leigh's book had been out for seven months, and not once during that time—or during his dozens of interviews with me— had Julian mentioned that the book might contain the password. Not once did he refer to it or try to put it right. Either he ignored it, as he does so many pressing issues, because he can't be bothered, is not diligent, thinks things will go away just because he wants them to, or—my personal belief—he never read Leigh's book, only excerpts fed to him by his colleagues or the Web. This would be unforgivable in any company member or security group, never mind one dealing in hundreds of thousands of secrets. But Julian is unsackable, and, like the unsackable all over the world, he makes decisions with the kind of hubris that trumps clear-sightedness and experience. There was no point in dumping those cables. By doing so, he risked exposing people mentioned in them. (No privacy is necessary, according to Julian, but he's wrong about that.) After he released all the cables, many of his allies turned against him. He had ruined the last of his reputation as a responsible publisher, just to get one over on *The Guardian*. I hung my head when I learned what he'd done, feeling it spelled long-term disaster for him.

I was getting a lot of calls asking me to speak about all this, but I didn't answer them. I'd failed not only to get the fascinating book I imagined, but to keep my involvement helpfully dark. The e-mails kept coming about doing a tell-all; they appeared to come from everywhere, and I froze. It wasn't just the usual reluctance to write too much, it was a sense of loyalty to my original idea of ghosting. Plus a kind of loyalty to Julian's vulnerability, especially (not in spite of) his role as enemy to himself. I just couldn't stand the scale of the errors he was making and didn't want to describe them. Not then. I knew it would take years and it has.

Jamie called to inform me they were about to tell Julian the book was going to be published. Canongate wanted to face down an attempted injunction before printing the book, not after. According to the lawyers, Julian had breached the contract, and if he injuncted they would fight for the right to publish. On September 7, 2011, a letter was sent to Julian telling him that "we will be publishing your autobiography this month and the book will be going to press on the 19th September . . . It will lack your formal imprimatur and you are entitled to distance yourself from our publication. However, in proceeding with publication under our original contract with you, the book will carry your copyright and we will honour your royalty payments once our costs have been recovered."

Julian called me in Glasgow and I spoke to him in a lane off Renfield Street. It was hard to hear what he was saying, but he was ranting against Canongate and saying he would seek an injunction. I already knew from Caroline Michel that he and WikiLeaks were in financial trouble and that he could not afford this—in the UK you have to prove to the judge that you can afford the costs if you lose. "But you've had the manuscript since April," I said, "and you did nothing about it."

"No. I've been trying to contact Jamie for weeks," he said. "And he wouldn't return the calls. He's obviously been planning this since early in the summer."

Lawyers' letters were exchanged.

I tried to convince Julian that legal steps would not work. It might be better to get hold of the book and make any crucial changes before it was too late. I said I could help him do this—to ensure that he was less vulnerable to attack or prosecution. I told him I had already redacted the names of the journalists who had been identified by him but whose side of the story Julian hadn't accounted for. We agreed on two areas where the manuscript might endanger him: first, on the issue of Chelsea Manning. He insisted "alleged source" be placed before Manning's name and I said I would pass that on. And second, the whole Swedish chapter would have to be looked at with a view to protecting his case there. "Spend the next day or two looking through the manuscript making amendments," I said. "And give them to me, and I'll force Canongate to make the changes. It's your best course of action."

"We might try both. We might try this method and an injunction," he said. But I knew this would require more effort than he was ever going to put in. His default position was to let the whole thing run out of control and then get into a Twitter war with the parties afterward.

"If you don't do this marking," I said, "and if you disappear into your bubble, there is nothing we can do to fix this. They will publish the book as it is."

"Okay," he said. "I agree." He then did nothing and made no marks to the manuscript.

I eventually told Jamie he should be ready to make some changes and it would then be possible to get Julian onside. "That should be fine," he said.

Julian asked me if I could get the Swedish chapter of the book sent to Helena Kennedy, who was by now advising him on a number of legal issues. I said I would try, and I asked Caroline to put pressure on Jamie. I also asked Jamie. He said he thought that would be fine. But Jamie was keen to protect his publication and the rights of those to whom he had sold it. Understandably, he wouldn't put up with further delays and wouldn't pass on the manuscript unless Julian agreed to sign a letter saying he wouldn't oppose the book. Julian was resisting this and preparing for war. I called Jamie: "You don't want his changes, do you?"

"At this stage I don't trust him to make them."

"That's fair enough. You won't have a book before Christmas. But I can see you wouldn't be convinced by anybody, not Leo Tolstoy himself, to delay the book."

"No, we couldn't. It's gone too far and he's had too many chances. We're publishing the book and this is the book we want to publish."

Geoffrey Robertson was then hired by Julian to check the book, completely missing the point that Canongate was about to push the button. There wasn't time.

On September 19 Canongate set the presses rolling. "We're proud of the book and he left us no choice but to publish," Jamie said. Caroline was engaged in a last-minute effort to stop publication, but even at this crucial stage her client was barely returning her calls.

Word was leaking out. Before I went to bed I saw messages on my phone from Nick Cohen at *The Observer* and several from *The Scotsman*. There was a text from Esther Addley of *The Guardian*. Jamie said someone at Waterstone's had phoned *The Guardian* to say they had a copy of the book. *The Independent* put a story online. Jamie had arranged for them—and the BBC's *Today* program—to have an exclusive the next morning, with the paper running two extracts, naming me as the writer and suggesting I'd bowed out of the project after feeling "uncomfortable" with the way things were going. I immediately turned my phone off.

The National Theatre of Scotland's adaptation of my book *The Missing* had opened in Glasgow that week. After the curtain one night, Jamie met me in the theater bar. He said he wanted me to get the first copy of the book. Holding it, I realized I felt nothing. I didn't feel it was by me, and the ghost's prerogative, to live a half-life in a house that wasn't mine, was all I had.

"We should seek maximum publicity and maximum debunking," Julian said the next day, "and I think both things can be done at the same time."

"How?" I said.

"By making as much publicity as possible; the book will sell. This is good. And by showing that the publishers jumped early, when we were working on a first draft, we can question the book's authority. We will choose five inaccuracies in the book and thereby invalidate its integrity. We will say you oppose the book . . ."

"Hold on," I said. "I'm not comfortable with that. I am not willing to be a pawn in this. The book was at an early stage and you didn't make changes. This is a matter between you and them, and it won't work to tell people I simply disapprove. It is not of any account whether I approve or not. I did my work, and Canongate will say, rightly, that you did not."

"That doesn't matter. Readers won't care about that. The thing to communicate is that we were on a journey that was interrupted." He said he was writing a press release and would send it to me. An e-mail came via the *London Review of Books*, from *The Wall Street Journal*, asking me to speak about what had happened. *The Sunday Times Magazine* left a message that I could have the cover to say whatever I wanted to say. During the evening, Julian, through his Twitter account, sent a bizarre message about truth being stranger than fiction, linking his followers to the book's Amazon page. Later that night he sent a "statement"—

i.e., a rant—to the Associated Press. Jamie Byng was staying in the spare room of the Glasgow flat, and I could hear him up in the night responding to texts and messages. In the morning, he told me he had been seeking the advice of Liz Sich at Colman Getty, the PR firm. He was white with rage about the allegations of misconduct directed at him by Julian in his statement.

> I have learned today through an article in the *Independent* that my publisher, Canongate, has secretly distributed an unauthorised 70,000-word first draft of what was going to be my autobiography . . . I am not "the writer" of this book. I own the copyright of the manuscript, which was written by Andrew O'Hagan. By publishing this draft against my wishes Canongate has acted in breach of contract, in breach of confidence, in breach of my creative rights and in breach of personal assurances . . . This book was meant to be about my life's struggle for justice through access to knowledge. It has turned into something else. The events surrounding its unauthorised publication by Canongate are not about freedom of information—they are about old-fashioned opportunism and duplicity—screwing people over to make a buck.
>
> On 20 December 2010, three days after being released from prison and while under house arrest, I signed a contract with Canongate and U.S. publisher Knopf. In it I agreed to authorise a 100,000–150,000 word book—part memoir, part manifesto— in order to fund legal defences and to contribute towards WikiLeaks' operating costs. On the 7th of December 2010 Bank of America, Visa, MasterCard, PayPal and Western Union folded to U.S. pressure by arbitrarily and unlawfully cutting WikiLeaks off of its financial lifeline. The blockade continues . . . My legal defence fund was similarly targeted and closed.
>
> The draft is published under the title *Julian Assange: The*

Unauthorised Autobiography—a contradiction in terms. It is a narrative and literary interpretation of a conversation between the writer and me. Although I admire Mr O'Hagan's writing, this draft was a work in progress. It is entirely uncorrected or fact-checked by me. The entire book was to be heavily modified, extended and revised, in particular, to take into account the privacy of the individuals mentioned in the book. I have a close friendship with Andrew O'Hagan and he stands by me.

The publisher has not been given a copy of the manuscript by Andrew O'Hagan or me. Rather, as a courtesy they were shown the "manuscript in progress" by Andrew O'Hagan's researcher, as an act of generosity, and for viewing purposes only—expressly agreed to by Canongate. Canongate physically took the manuscript, kept it, and did not return it to Mr O'Hagan or me.

Contrary to what the *Independent* reports, I did not pull the plug on the deal, nor was I unwilling to compromise. Rather, I proposed on 7 June 2011 to cancel the contract as it stood in order to write up a fresh contract with a new deadline. I informed the publishers . . . having explained that with the upcoming extradition appeal in the High Court and an ongoing espionage Grand Jury against me in Virginia, I was not in a position to dedicate my full attention to a book that would narrate my personal story and my life's work. On 9 June 2011 I received an e-mail from my agency, PFD, informing me that the U.S. and UK publishers (Knopf and Canongate) were interested in renegotiating the form of the book, and insisting on cancelling the contract as it stood . . . It is this contract, that had been agreed to be cancelled by all parties, that Canongate is basing its actions on.

In a meeting on 20 May 2011 with Canongate publisher Jamie

Byng, I verbally agreed to deliver the agreed 100,000–150,000 word manuscript by the end of the year. In a recorded phone conversation on (or the day before or after) 15 June 2011, Jamie Byng gave me assurances that Canongate would never, contrary to rumours given to me, publish the book without my consent. We would agree to restructure the book and the deadline, and draw up a new contract. In correspondence (24 August 2011) my agent wrote: "We are going to arrange for you to have a one-to-one meeting with Jamie" . . . However, Jamie Byng ignored my agent's attempts to arrange a meeting with me. My agent then informed me that Jamie Byng would refuse to take any of my calls. Despite this I and two members of my team tried repeatedly to contact him . . . During all this time we were unaware of Canongate's secret plan to publish the manuscript without consent.

On 7 September, Canongate informed my agent that they wanted to print the unauthorised book Monday, 19 September 2011. I was advised by my lawyers that I had grounds for obtaining a *quia timet* injunction to prevent the printing . . . on the basis that the proposal amounts to an infringement of copyright, a breach of the agreement, plus a breach of my right not to have my work subjected to derogatory treatment.

On 16 September 2011, I wrote a letter to my publisher informing them of my intention to obtain a temporary injunction unless they agreed to make immediately available to QC Geoffrey Robertson a copy of the proposed book. In keeping with my rights under the contract, I requested five days for legal review of the manuscript by my own barrister, so that he could suggest any deletions reasonably required to protect our people from any adverse legal consequences that may arise from this publication. Jamie Byng attempted to extort legal immunity for his actions by refusing to give me even a single chapter of the book unless I signed away my right to take legal action against Canongate . . .

One of Julian's techniques, again borrowed from the spymasters he purports to find criminal, is to tape conversations with friends and colleagues and then use them to "prove" duplicity. My interviews with him were recorded contemporaneously, either on tape or in notes, and I had tapes running and notepads in my hand all the time I was with him. But his use of private recordings with Canongate seemed to me a new low. As for me, the statement that I "supported him," that I was his friend, etc., was out of order. He was using me. It was against my consistent wish that I not be dragged into the middle of this dispute. But in this dispute Julian considered everybody but himself a pawn. He was the king we were all obliged to protect. The fact was I supported Julian where I could, but I often couldn't, and he knew it. I tried to give him as much encouragement as I could, seeing his point of view and all that, and I continued to do so, but my arguments with him were all in the open. The morning after Julian's press release, Jamie wanted me to refute Julian's claims and I said that he was just doing the same thing as Julian. I would tell my own version when the time was right but my role in this was to be silent. Did any of them understand that?

I got the 6:30 a.m. train to London. The steward offered me a copy of *The Independent*. Front-page headline: EXCLUSIVE EXTRACTS: JULIAN ASSANGE, THE UNAUTHORISED AUTOBIOGRAPHY. Giant splash. Inside, the story went on to say that I had become "uncomfortable about the furore" around Julian and his publishers and implied that this was why I'd decided that my name "will not appear on the memoir." Nonsense:

at my insistence, my name was never intended to appear on the book. I put my headphones on. *Today* program, Nick Davies of Canongate: "We gave him a number of opportunities. We took the co-writer off the project."

Having told me on the phone that he would covertly try to boost sales of the book and then not-too-covertly posting a link to its Amazon page on Twitter, Julian called again while I was standing in the corridor of King's College London on Friday, September 23. He said that maybe the book should be published in America after all. "We could call it 'the Authorized Version,'" he said. I laughed. But later he started to campaign against the book. Jamie felt outraged by the untruths and distortions in Julian's account, and sat down to write an open letter to him. On the advice of Colman Getty, the letter was never sent, but it was scathing and convincing. It pointed out that Julian delivered nothing and that he was breaching my wish to remain anonymous and that he should wait for my statement, one day, of what actually happened. It also stated that all advance money was paid to him via his lawyer and what happened to the money after that was nothing to do with Canongate.

Julian's late-night online campaign had the usual effect of turning a bad patch into a vipers' nest. He never really apologized to anyone, but got busy turning his publishers into the latest enemy, to go alongside Daniel Domscheit-Berg, Mark Stephens, *The Guardian*, *The New York Times*, my researcher, his former host at Ellingham Hall, the government of Australia, his activist friends in Iceland, and a host of others who'd dared to have their own views. There would be many more to come: Jemima Khan, *The Big Issue*, Barack Obama, and Assange's own political party in Australia. I stayed on good terms with him as long as I did only because I kept quiet.

He hadn't wanted the book not to sell—vanity operates in

odd ways—but the effect of his campaign was to hurt sales. And yet he couldn't stop, going out of his way to distribute transcripts of private phone calls between him and Jamie and publishing e-mails that he claimed showed Canongate's trickiness. I wanted to warn him that they certainly had transcripts of our interviews (due to our pressing deadline, they'd helped me transcribe some of them), sittings in which he'd uttered, late at night, many casual libels, many sexist or anti-Semitic remarks, and where he spoke freely about every aspect of his life. There was little security consciousness at work in those interviews, and I calmed them down when preparing the manuscript and removed things that were said in the heat of the moment or that were too much or too jocular or just banter, but Canongate could have released them to the press at any time, rubbishing his notion that he did not want a "memoir" and devastating him in his own words. I have those tapes still and they can be shocking. Canongate didn't retaliate or wound him. Like me, they imagined he was under pressure and hoped that, through a combination of tolerance and care in the community, he would eventually stop all this and return to the work that had made him so interesting in the first place. "Why don't you go after some baddies," I said to Julian, "and stop fighting with the people on your side?"

And here's the hard bit. Those of us who grew up in the 1980s and 1990s, especially in the United Kingdom under Thatcher and Blair, those of us who lived through the Troubles and the Falklands War, the miners' strike, the deregulation of the City, and Iraq, believed that exposing secret deals and covert operations would prove a godsend. When WikiLeaks began this process in 2010, it felt, to me anyhow, but also to many others, that this might turn out to be the greatest contribution to democracy since the end of the Cold War. A new kind of openness suddenly looked possible: technology might allow people to watch their watchers, at last, and to inspect the secrets being kept, supposedly in our name, and to expose fraud and exploitation wherever it was encountered in the new media age. It wasn't a subtle plan but it smacked of the kind of idealism that many of us hadn't felt for a while in British life, where big moral programs on the left are thin on the ground. Assange looked like a counterwarrior and a man not made for the deathly compromises of party politics. And he seemed deeply connected to the Web's powers of surveillance and countersurveillance. What happened, though, is that government opposition to WikiLeaks's work—which continues— became confused, not least in Assange's mind, with the rape accusations against him. It has been a fatal conflation. There's a distinct lack of clarity in Julian's approach, a lack that is, I'm afraid, only reinforced by the people he has working with him. When he heard I was writing this he sent me an e-mail saying it was illegal for me to speak out without what he called "appropriate consultation" with him. He wrote of his precarious situation and of the FBI investigation into his activities. "I have been detained," he said, "without charge, for 1000 days." And there it is, the old conflation, implying that his detention is to do with his work against secret-keepers in America. It is not. He was detained at Ellingham Hall while appealing against a request to extradite him to Sweden to answer questions relating to two rape allegations. A man who conflates such truths loses his moral authority right there: I tried to spell this out to him while writing the book, but he wouldn't listen, sometimes suggesting I was naïve not to consider the rape allegations to have been a "honey trap" set by dark foreign forces, or that the Swedes were merely keen to extradite him to America. Because he has no ability to see through other people's eyes he can't see how dishonest this conflation seems even to supporters such as me. It was a trap he built for himself when he refused to go to Sweden and instead went into the embassy of a nation not famous for its respect for freedom of speech. (He moved there in August 2012, when I was still seeing him, and the book was over.) He will always have an answer to these points. But there is no real answer. He made a massive tactical error in not going to Sweden to clear his name.

Up to the time of writing, I did nothing to break with him or unsettle him. I have watched the collapse of a dozen good relationships he had, and tried to discuss them with him, assuaging him much more than I probably should have. I resisted him firmly when he overstepped the mark—by telling me, for instance, that all my taped interviews with him should be destroyed—but I tried a different tack from the others, making myself available to him in the belief that he needed someone outside his immediate circle as he attempted to fight the forces that threatened him, including himself, and get back to his work. That is why I took so long to say what I'm saying now: I knew the truth would hurt him because the truth, after all, was not his friend. It takes a bigger person than Julian to see what they did wrong, and many of us, including several of those who stood bail for him, hung back and continued to flatter him with our tolerance. When Jemima Khan publicly broke with him, he didn't pause to ask why a loyal supporter might become aggrieved; when I raised it with him he simply made a horribly sexist remark.

He began living in the Ecuadorian embassy a gestative nine months after the autobiography debacle had come to its end. When I first went to see him there he was in a corner room at the back of the embassy, surrounded by hampers from Harrods across the way—well-wishers' presents to the incarcerated—and sitting at a grubby desk covered in snacks and papers. A running machine stood along one wall. He told me about a failed siege by the police and about some projects they were getting off the ground, but quickly, as always, turned to demolishing one of his supporters. He continued with his habit of biting the hand that fed him, satirizing or undermining those who came to his aid. He said the Ecuadorian ambassador was mad and "stalked the corridor." He said she thought she was fat and went on a ludicrous diet because she didn't like the way she looked in the photographs taken by the *Daily Mail*. I was nice to him, too nice, asking him what I could do, and mentioned again the Verso project and the idea of me helping them to get that going. He showed interest but you saw it fading in his eyes.

On another visit, again around midnight, he told me I shouldn't tell the police at the door of the embassy my name. "I didn't," I told him. "I'm not obliged to tell them my name."

"They're keeping a list of my visitors," he said. And then he asked if I'd heard of a film about him that was being planned by DreamWorks. I told him I had and that it was due to star Benedict Cumberbatch. I told him I knew Cumberbatch and that he was a good guy and a powerful actor. He talked about how the actor looked compared with how he looked. Sarah arrived and we laughed about some of the Ellingham Hall absurdities and all the things that had happened since then. Julian had lost all those appeals that had so preoccupied him, but was no less preoccupied and no less time-wasting. He was obsessing about the Dream-Works film and said it was bound to be a smear. He said he could get to see the script—presumably by hacking into someone's e-mail—but that he wouldn't agree to Cumberbatch's request for an interview because it would appear he was endorsing the film. Cumberbatch wrote to Julian repeatedly and was met with a friendly but hectoring attempt to stop the film they wanted to make. In the end, Julian wanted editorial control and I reminded him that creative people, including creative writers, could not be

stopped from going their own way. Cumberbatch was sensitive
to the problems, but he wasn't going to be bullied. I could never
fathom the distance between Julian's idealism, on the one hand,
and his wish to exploit vulnerability, on the other. The film, like
the book, would serve to remind people of the important work
he had, at his best, been trying to do. But Julian just worried
about his enemies and how they would "use" the ambivalences
that any decent artist would bring to such a contradictory figure.
His contradictions could rock you off your feet. He called me
one day during the making of the DreamWorks movie, when I
was in a supermarket in Camberwell. "I've got an idea," he said.
"They'll want you as a consultant on this film. Why don't you say
yes to that, and split the fee with me?"

"Because I'm not interested in that," I said, "and if you want
to oppose the film, why would you also want to make a profit
from it?"

"Why not?" he said.

He sometimes seems like a cornered animal in the embassy.
One day he asked me to come in to talk to him. As soon as I entered the room, a new, bigger room but standard-issue, messy,
depressing, smelling of laborious boring hours, I could see he
was disturbed about something. "I've received some intelligence that you're preparing a book," he said. "That you have tapes
and you're going to talk about visiting me here in the middle of
the night." I told him I'd made no plans to write a book, and had,
as he knew, turned down massive offers to do so. I reminded him
I was a writer and that one day I might, and that it was normal
for people to speculate about it. "Just tell me first if you're going
to," he said. "Come to me first."

I said I would. And I said many conciliatory things without
really believing them anymore. His burst of distrust had shown
me he would only ever see me as a servant, and in that moment

the account I'm writing here became a reality. He did what he was now famous for doing, building the creature he most feared would come to get him, and I left that night in the knowledge that my time with him, over snowy nights and long crazy afternoons of denial, had brought me back to first position, as a writer. He was a character. It didn't matter to me now whether he continued the work he'd started or stayed true to what he said. He was a figure out of Dostoyevsky, a figure out of James Hogg or John Banville, and a figure most vitally out of me. I was now making him into a figment of my imagination and that was perhaps all he could ever really be for me. Sitting in that prison of his own peculiar making, Julian was by then a cipher, a person whose significance can scarcely be grasped by himself, though he is forced to live with it. Planet Julian was now the site of at least a dozen little implosions every month. His 2013 bid for the Australian senate as chairman of the WikiLeaks Party was a fiasco, not least because of the kind of inattention I had come to know so well. "Attending one out of the thirteen national council meetings of the party," the council member Daniel Mathews said as he resigned, "is a fairly low participation rate in one's own party."

There were two last visits. During the first I was led in by a new young assistant, Ethan, who was keen to agree with everything being said. Our conversation was mainly about Edward Snowden. There are few subjects on which Julian would be reluctant to take what you might call a paternalistic position, but over Snowden, whom he's never met but has chatted with and feels largely responsible for, he expressed a kind of irritable admiration. "Just how good is he?" I asked.

"He's number nine," he said.

"In the world? Among computer hackers? And where are you?"

"I'm number three." He went on to say that he wondered whether Snowden was calm enough, intelligent enough, and added that he should have come to them for advice before fleeing to Hong Kong.

A fair reading of the situation might conclude, without prejudice, that Julian, like an aging movie star, was a little put out by the global superstardom of Snowden. He has always cared too much about the fame and too much about the credit, while real relationships and real action often fade to nothing. Snowden was now the central hub and Julian was keen to help him and keen to be seen helping him. It's how the ego works, and the ego always comes first. Snowden, while grateful for the advice and the comradeship, was meanwhile playing a cannier game than Julian. He was eager for credit, too, but behaving more subtly, more amiably, and playing with bigger secrets. Julian said he hoped that others—I took him to mean *The Guardian* and Glenn Greenwald—didn't claim too much credit for the flow of secrets. He said he wanted me to help him get a film going, an account of what actually happened in Hong Kong, how he helped Snowden. He said he had all the inside information and connections and it would make a fantastic thriller. We discussed it at length and I told him the way to get movie interest in such a thing was to get behind a big piece in *Vanity Fair*. He agreed and said he would set aside time to get down to it. But I knew he wouldn't. It was odd the way he spoke about Snowden, almost jealously, as if the younger man didn't quite understand what he was about, needing much more from Julian than he knew how to ask for. I recognized the familiar anxiety about noninfluence: "Snowden should have been with us from the beginning," he said. "He's flailing." But they were now making up for lost time. As we spoke, Sarah was in Moscow Airport, where Snowden was being held without a passport. "I sent Sarah over," said Julian in his favorite mode. All he needed at that point was a white cat to stroke.

Snowden was everywhere in the news the last time I decided to drop in on Julian after I'd been out in his neighborhood. The embassy was quiet. I brought a couple of bottles of beer up from the street and we sat in the dark room. It was a Friday night and Julian had never seemed more alone. We laughed a lot and then he went very deeply into himself. He drank his beer and then lifted mine and drank that. "We've got some really historic things going on," he said. Then he opened his laptop and the blue screen lit his face and he hardly noticed me leaving.

The Invention of
Ronald Pinn

first went to Camberwell New Cemetery about six years ago, looking for the grave of a young man called Melvin Bryan, a petty criminal who died after being stabbed at a drug house in the London area of Edmonton. Walking down the pathways and over the crisp, frozen leaves, I'd noticed how many of the people buried there had died young—you can often pick them out by the soft toys resting against the gravestones. Last winter I came back to the same place. It was even colder this time, and the pathways were glittering as I made my way down to the church. I hadn't taken in before that Charlie Richardson, leader of the Richardson Gang, was buried here, as well as George Cornell, the gangster shot by the Kray Twins in the Blind Beggar pub. But it was the graves and sentry toys of the unknown children that had lodged in my mind. The trees were bare, filtering light on the tombstones and pointing down at the stories gathered there. When I say "stories," I don't only mean the ones clinging to the gravestones, but the stories you come with, the tales you tell yourself and that don't yet have a particular meaning. For some reason not yet clear to me, I noted down the names of Paul Ives, Graham Paine ("who lost his life by drowning"), Clifford John Dunn, Ronald Alexander Pinn, and John Hill, all of whom were born in the 1960s, as I was, and died early.

The practice of using dead children's identities began in the

Metropolitan Police in the 1960s. Until very recently, it was thought, in-house, to be a legitimate part of an undercover officer's tradecraft. It involved taking a child's name from a gravestone or a register and building what the police called a "legend" around it. When I first heard about it, I wondered if the officers involved in this activity were not in fact covert novelists, giving their "characters" a hinterland that suited the purpose of their present investigations, as well as a false passport and a new face. The Met officers, without informing the families of the children, and using their original birth certificates, each built a profile that would pass for an actual person. And as such—as actual people—these police officers infiltrated left-wing groups, posing as activists. In 2013 several officers who had engaged in this activity on behalf of the Met's Special Demonstration Squad (SDS), including Sergeant John Dines, admitted to using the identities of dead children to conceal their own identities. Dines took the name of John Barker, who died of leukemia in 1968, at the age of eight. In several of the cases, officers kept their fake identities for more than ten years and exploited them in sexual situations. To strengthen their "backstory," they would visit the places of their "childhood," walking around the houses they had lived in before they died, all the better to implant the legend of their second life.

Mick Creedon, the chief constable of Derbyshire, reporting a few years ago as part of Operation Herne, an inquiry into the activities of the SDS, stated that 106 covert identities had been "identified as having been used by the SDS between 1968 and 2008," and confirmed that many of those identities had been "fictitious." For reasons of "operational security," the chief constable would not confirm or deny the names of specific dead children or specific police officers. There was no moral questioning. The report was forced into existence by bad press, and, though the police made apologies, we were left with no real sense of what exactly had been done. The situation said a lot about the power of the police, and the power of the media to move the police to apology. Yet the story went deeper than that. What was it to live a second life? What was it to use a person's identity—and did anyone own it in the first place? Is it the spirit of the present age, that in the miasma of social media everyone's "truth" is exploitable, especially by themselves? Is the line between the real and the fictional fixed, and could I cross the line of my own inquiry and do the police in different voices? Could I take a dead young man's name and see how far I could go in animating a fake life for him? How wrong would it be to go on such a journey and do what these men had done? I chose to get at the conundrum by pursuing Ronald Pinn into the fantastical dimensions of a future life he didn't live. If the task ahead turned on an outrageous defilement of a person's identity, then that, too, would be part of the story I was trying to tell. But the costs were real. An immersion in wrongdoing and illegality would be necessary to tell it from the absolute center.

RONALD ALEXANDER PINN

"Ronnie"
DIED 9.8.1984
Aged 20 years

My happy handsome son,
I pray for the day when we meet again,
All my love, Mum

I had no idea as I left the cemetery that evening how far beyond the police's bad behavior the story would go; that it would be about the ghostliness of the Internet and the way we live with it. But I remember putting on my car headlamps and watching the yellow light pick out the graves, and I stayed there for a while thinking about the fictions I had grown up with.

The real Ronald Pinn was born on January 23, 1964. His mother's name was Glenys Lilian Evans and she came from the area around the Old Kent Road. His father grew up in the same part of London and was working as a builder when Ronnie was born. In that year, they lived at 183 St. James's Road in Bermondsey. British Pathé footage shot on the Old Kent Road during the 1970s shows children on the streets, and early in my search, I used to scan the little groups playing by building sites or standing at bus stops, the children under the advertising hoardings or walking past the shops, to see if any of them resembled a blond-haired boy in a photo on a family tree, a boy that a family research website told me was Ronnie Pinn.

That photo was the only evidence of Ronald Pinn's existence in the public domain: a blurred and fuzzy image of a person hardly anyone still remembered. Other than that, Ronald Pinn had never existed, and neither had any of his family. There were no reports, nothing from any newspapers, no certificates, no records, and no social media footprint to measure. Just this single, blurred photo. I began to wonder if paperwork or old-fashioned memory might have preserved what the Internet disdained, but everyday material that hasn't been digitized and has no fame value is increasingly hard to find. I wrote to all the people in all the school classes that might have been attended by Ronnie Pinn. I wrote to all the Pinns in London. And only slowly did one or two emerge from the non-digital ether, the old-fashioned air, to tell me what they remembered of him. His family had lived in Avondale Square, just off the Old Kent Road, and I went to see the tired old flats down there. I could see him playing on the grassy mound in the hot summer of 1976 when he was twelve. I could see him shouting up to his mother standing on the balcony and parking his Chopper bicycle by the trees under the flats. And often I realized it wasn't Ronnie I was seeing: I was seeing myself, a boy of similar age who somehow knew those places well, and hung about in the unrecorded life.

Ronnie went to Sir John Cass's Foundation Primary School, a Church of England school not far from the Tower of London, but nobody remembers him there. I saw some photographs of boys on an outing to Stonehenge; it was the right period, but Ronnie wasn't pictured. Pupils remembered other people and they remembered the school's routines, such as walking in twos to St. Botolph's in Aldgate to take part in church services. Ronnie's mother hadn't liked the look of the primary school near where they were living, so he made the journey each day to Sir John Cass's, and he was happy there if not commemorated in any way. Former pupils at Bacon's Secondary School in Bermondsey still talk about the famous people who went there, but nobody noticed that, after primary school, Ronnie Pinn was there, too, until 1980. In my hunt for the real Ronnie, I thought several times that I saw him in grainy photos posted by ex-pupils on Friends Reunited. Was he not the boy in the white shirt at the edge of a photograph taken in front of the school in 1980, with kids tumbling over each other and somebody spraying from a shook-up can?

He tended to do well in class but on a report card for July 1978 you can see things were changing. His attendance was dropping and he had four detentions. He got A's in math and drama, but did less well in English and got a D in French ("Ronald made very little progress this year"). He got an A in metalwork, but the teacher couldn't think of his name and wrote "Robert" while telling him to keep up the good work. His form teacher, Mr. Norman, said, "Ronnie's attitude and standard of work is slipping. I hope that he takes note of what has been said to him recently. He is always pleasant and happy." Ronnie seemed like a person ready for the world outside and he left school as soon as he was allowed to. Someone remembered him on a trip to Wales: "Ronnie said he was in the dorm when a little boy came and sat on the end of his bed in the middle of the night, a boy dressed in old-fashioned clothes. Then he disappeared." The person who told me this then sighed. "I think Ronnie was born to die. I mean, we all are, but him especially."

Ronnie met a girl, Nicola Searle, whose family worked the market stalls just outside London, and he started working with them. That was his life for a time, a certain amount of ducking and diving in the stallholders' world. Eventually he bought a Golf soft-top car, and he idolized it. He wasn't ambitious. He went on nights out and he bought some suits and took the occasional line of cocaine. It was the early 1980s and boys like Ronnie were popping up in the City and making new selves for themselves. But Ronnie seemed happy to stick with the same small group of friends in South London. Sometime in 1983, his girlfriend broke up with him and took up with a guy they both knew called Coxy. Ronnie couldn't understand it—the guy turned out to be no good—but he found another girl, Sharon, "a girl with legs up to here," he said, and people insist he would have married her. The breakup was awkward because he was still living in a flat he'd leased from Nicola's family, high up in a block in Cotton Gardens, halfway down Kennington Lane.

It was a Thursday, the day he died. He had a habit of ringing his mother every day but she hadn't heard from him that week. She went looking for him, and, after asking around, found his car in a side street off the Tower Bridge Road. She couldn't understand why he would leave his car there and she went in search of him. (It appears he abandoned his car and walked home.) At a pub near Avondale Square she met a friend of Ronnie's called David. He said he'd been with Ronnie the day before and that Ronnie was in bed the last time he saw him. (The coroner would later describe this man as an "unsavoury witness" without detailing why.) Mrs. Pinn, in company with another boy from the bar, went to the block of flats where Ronnie lived. She was nervous going up there because it just wasn't Ronnie to let days go by without ringing her to say hello, and her panic increased when they discovered his flat was locked from the inside. The caretaker and the young friend went to find another way in while Mrs. Pinn sat in a neighbor's flat.

When I first learned of the basic circumstances of Ronnie Pinn's death, I didn't know if his mother was alive. I was still looking through electoral rolls and writing letters to people who weren't her. She never believed Ronnie was a heroin addict. Was the heroin dose that killed him part of a life she didn't know about?

Inside the flat, Ronnie's trousers were folded over a chair by the bed. A wake-up call had been set on the phone right next to him. And his passport was there, showing stamps from a visit to Santiago de Compostela and a trip to America he'd made with an uncle when he was young. Everything was in its place in the flat. Ronnie lay dead, aged twenty, with nothing around him and few records attached to his name. He was gone. He had died not three miles from where he grew up, and, in the three decades to come, his name crossed only once onto the Internet, attached to that photograph of a boy on a distant family tree.

I went to meet a man at King's Cross Station who had gone to school with one of Ronnie's uncles. He showed me a picture and I could see the family resemblance, but the man couldn't remember Ronnie. And hardly anyone he went to school with could recall him either. In 2014, none of them knew that the remains of Ronald Pinn had lain in a cemetery in Camberwell for three decades. They all had children of their own and houses on which the mortgage was almost paid. They had reunions to attend and they would reminisce on ancestry websites about housing estates now swept away, about buses that no longer ran and music they'd forever associate with other lost boys.

My first step in trying to create a fake identity based on Ronald Pinn's was to apply for the real Ronnie's death and birth certificates. This is why the police and others use real young people who died: like the rest of us they have certificates that can form the basis of a credible story, but in their case there isn't a continuing life, or much life at all, to get in the way of the made-up story. I didn't know Ronnie's mother's maiden name at the time but I fudged that and easily got the certificates from the General Register Office. As in every case, the certificates begin a process of legitimization: if you have a birth certificate you can get other documents, and in this way a fake identity's "legend" is grounded. The real Ronnie's family background wasn't hard to establish from the certificates: his father died in 1997; his paternal grandfather, Alfred E. Pinn of Southwark, was born in 1908; his great-grandfather, a trader called Zenos Thomas Victor Pinn, died in Lambeth Hospital during the Second World War. I was able to establish the basic facts of Ronnie Pinn's background without any difficulty. People nowadays are often obsessed with ancestry, and records that used to take weeks to search are now visible in a matter of minutes, for a fee. At the same time, Facebook and other social media platforms encourage the opposite: the invented life. Writing this story, I moved continually from one way of knowing a person to another, from the real to the fictive, and it seemed a pretty contemporary way of understanding a life.

The day after I went to see the house the real Ronnie grew up in, the 1930s block in Avondale Square with grass at the front and children playing outside, I invented a real e-mail address for my fake Ronnie. Fictional characters have a habit of gathering material to themselves, and so it was with my invented Ronnie. I began to establish a background for him, a legend that touched on my own, while at the same time leaving the original Ronnie behind and forging new connections to a plausible self. I decided his family's address at the time of his birth would be 167 Caledonian Road, because the address seemed right in class terms for the man I was inventing and also because I have a feeling for King's Cross. I placed him at Blessed Sacrament Catholic Primary School in Boadicea Street, which, after visiting it, I gathered would have been a new school when "Ronnie" attended. Like a spy, I wanted my character to have a legend that was so copper-bottomed, so strong and sure, like Oliver Twist's, say, or Humbert Humbert's, or mine, that it wouldn't just fool the public but very nearly fool its author. I looked at old photographs from this school, and from the secondary school I placed him at, St. Aloysius College in Highgate, and inserted him in group photographs from the 1970s, after St. Aloysius became a comprehensive. I matched his dates to real people who would have been at the school during those years, and saw that his first friends could have been Paul Ward, Brian Foster, and Terry Klepka.

Many of our modern crimes are crimes of the imagination. We think of the unspeakable and exchange information on it. We commit a "thought crime"—giving the illicit or the abominable an audience. Some of us pretend to have relationships we don't actually have just for the sense of freedom it gives us, and some want porn for that reason, too. Building the fake Ronnie became something more than creating a character in a novel: it became personal, like living another life, as an actor might, trying not only to imitate the experience of a possible person but testing how far I could develop a sense of reality and empathy for him. And I found I did: I had feelings about my invented Ronnie, and I cared about how he seemed. I decided my Ronnie, unlike the real one, would have gone to university, and I placed him at Edinburgh from 1982 to 1986. I applied for a fake degree certificate in his name—there are several websites offering this service, all of them pretending the certificates are for "novelty value only," but they look as real as the originals, have identical seals, holograms, and watermarks, and can sell for thousands of pounds. They are clearly meant for people who want to pretend they have a degree that they don't have. Edinburgh seemed right: I knew how to think as Ronnie in the Edinburgh of those years.

I realized my Ronnie would need a face. He would need it more for identity cards than for his online life, though even there it seems wrong after a while not to have a face to represent the self you are projecting to the world. I could have lifted an age-appropriate face—the chances of detection would have been slight. But I was uneasy about that: I suspected my Ronnie might travel into some dark areas, and I wanted it to be me who was to blame, or at least responsible, so the face of a real person, alive or dead, was out. Through a friend in the film business, I contacted a special-effects guy and over tea in Portland Place I swore him to secrecy. The conversation about how my man would look turned into something like a casting session. "I think he should look like me, but not too much," I told him, and we agreed he'd make several images of a face that blended mine with those of two other men who agreed to sit for portraits. Ronnie's face would then be a mixture of the three. My special-effects helper asked me if I'd heard of Weavrs.

"What's that?"

"It's where you're going," he said. According to its website, Weavrs are "personality-based social-web robots" that "publicly blog about how they feel, where they go and what they experience." An article by Olivia Solon in *Wired* magazine questioned the guys behind it. "The team . . . won't reveal exactly how the Weavrs algorithm works—referring to it as their black box," Solon wrote, "but say they create personalities from social data that then 'blog themselves into existence.'" It's taken for granted in these circles that digital robots are becoming a tool of big business; in China, for instance, Weavrs are used to collect data on young people and their preferences. In the old days researchers would speak to individuals, but nowadays the invented person, the digividual, is more reliable when it comes to showing what people want.

The unstable factor is "people." My Ronnie Pinn had integrity at his source, a real person who lived and breathed and was called Ronnie Pinn, but he himelf had none, which didn't stop him from beginning to live a life much larger than reality. The photograph of "Ronnie" showed a man in his forties with his author's eyes and a younger man's haircut. He was a composite yet he seemed quite ordinary—everyone, after all, is a composite—and nothing about him suggested he wasn't walking in the world like us. My Ronnie was soon set up on Facebook, with his photo uploaded and his background details included, his "education," his football team (West Ham), and the fact that he now worked as a driver for a firm called Executive Cars. It was at this point that Ronnie's "character" began to veer off on its own, as characters do when you're creating them in fiction. Ronnie, it turned out, was quite right wing, he was gay, he was a historian who'd turned his back on academia and wanted England out of Europe. On

Facebook, he expressed his character in his choice of people and institutions to follow. He liked fast food, so, for a while, he had a logo of Wendy's on his page. He had Wembley Stadium as the background on his home page. Every day I added new elements to him and found new avenues. He liked *Star Trek*, *The Wire*, and *Queer as Folk*. He joined Twitter and started following certain monarchists, capitalists, fast-food outlets, and old school connections, as well as politicians like Nigel Farage. People automatically started following Ronnie Pinn, either because of his interests or because he followed them. But to increase his footprint I kept adding more possibilities, including a host of fake Facebook friends. They were like ghosts and I came to think of them as figments, the invented, the others, who shored up the legend of a fake person by being plausibly real while being totally fake. In less than an hour one morning the invented friends of Ronnie Pinn came into being. They had names like William Eliot, Jane Deleon, and Stephen Watley, and who's to say they weren't "real." After a while, an alarm bell went off somewhere, and Facebook sent a warning. "Please verify your identity," it said. "Facebook does not allow accounts that: Pretend to be someone else; Use a fake name; Don't represent a real person." But the fakery of the fake Ronnie's fake friends didn't trouble them for long. It was just another robot sending the warning, moved to do so after a number of keystrokes set off the alarm. But the fakery continued to go deeper and Ronnie Pinn grew in reality and the warnings disappeared. At the time, Facebook had 864 million daily users, of whom at least 67 million are believed by the company to be fake. There are more social media ghosts, more people being second people, or living an invented life as doppelgängers, than there are citizens of the UK.

In many ways my Ronnie was a typical twenty-first-century citizen. Not least in his falseness. Valuable fake identities are being constructed and deployed in every area of life, and often they are simulacra of their maker's own identity. In a 2013 book called *Murdoch's World* by David Folkenflik, it emerged that public relations staffers at Fox News Channel were serially creating dummy accounts to plant "Fox-friendly" reactions to critical blog postings. One ex-staffer spoke of more than a hundred false accounts set up for this purpose, and said they'd covered their tracks by the use of different computers and untraceable broadband connections. Far from being the creations of stoned computer nerds, fake online identities had long since become a standard feature of big-business espionage, police investigations, government surveillance, marketing, and public relations. Democracy itself— with its basic notion of one individual and one vote—is far from being an innocent notion in the age of "astroturfing," when whole movements of opinion can be manufactured in an instant, drummed up by the keyboard-savvy, who harvest "names" from social media to support their cause or denounce someone else's. Edward Snowden opened a door on state-sponsored snooping on private lives, but also, more subtly, he revealed the many ways private life has given itself over to the dark arts of fabrication. A dirty tricks document produced by a secret unit in British Intelligence called JTRIG (Joint Threat Research Intelligence Group) was called "The Art of Deception: Training for a New Generation of Online Covert Operations." JTRIG described itself as "using online techniques to make something happen in the real or the cyber world." Making "something happen" very often means invading someone's Facebook account and changing the photographs, or mobilizing the social network to ridicule them. A "fake flag operation," for example, involves posting material on the Internet under a false identity with the aim of damaging a reputation. The damage comes under one of two headings: "Dissimulation— Hide the Real" and "Simulation—Show the False." In other words, exploit the porousness of the border between the real and the imagined, as if some Borgesian nightmare had taken over, feasting on a general uncertainty about who exists and who doesn't. The world, according to the British security organization GCHQ (Government Communication Headquarters), is now a zone of conjuring. "We want to build Cyber Magicians," the secret report tells its secret readers.

Stories of people pretending to be other people, of people feeling impelled to confect, imitate, or perform themselves, describe a change not just in the technological basis of our lives but in the narrative strategies now available to us. You could say that every ambitious person needs a legend to deepen their own. In 2013, Manti Te'o, an exceptional Hawaiian linebacker, a Mormon who played for Notre Dame, found his when he told the sad story of having to succeed for his team after his twenty-two-year-old girlfriend, Lennay Kekua, died of leukemia. Despite his grief, the football player stormed up the field, making twelve tackles in one game, before appearing on news programs to talk about his heartbreak and to quote from the letters Kekua had written him during her terrible illness. Problem was: the girlfriend never existed. She was a complete invention—the photographs on social media sites were of a Girl he'd never met. He hadn't made it to Kekua's funeral, Te'o said, because she insisted that he not miss the game. There are hundreds of stories like this, where "sock puppet" accounts on Facebook and elsewhere have allowed a "person"—sometimes a whole "family"—to put together a life that's much bigger than the real one. The Dirr family from Ohio solicited sympathy and dollars for years after losing loved ones to cancer—a small village of more than seventy invented profiles shored up the lie. It was all the work of a twenty-two-year-old medical student, Emily Dirr, who'd been inventing her world since she was eleven. Her life was a reality show that she produced, cast, directed, starred in, and broadcast to the world under a pile of aliases that felt entirely real and moving to a large group of devoted followers.

By the middle of the summer of 2014, Ronnie Pinn had a Gmail account and an AOL account, as well as accounts on Craigslist and Reddit. It took the best part of a week to install and run the software necessary to get the bitcoins he needed to confirm his existence. I bought them with a credit card—hundreds of pounds' worth—on computers that couldn't be traced back to me. In each case they had to be "mixed," or laundered, before Ronnie could buy things. Around every corner on the Web is a scam, and the Ronnie I invented had to negotiate with some of the dodgiest parts of the World Wide Web. He now had currency; next he got a fake address. I used an empty flat in Islington, where I would go to collect his mail, the emptiness of the hall seeming all the emptier for the pile of mail on the floor, addressed to someone who didn't exist but was more demanding than many who did.

It wasn't long before I saw Ronnie's face on a driving license. It took a few weeks to secure a passport. The seller was on the Dark Net website Evolution; having gathered all "Ronnie's" information, he produced scans on which the photographs were missing. Then he disappeared. This is common enough: the sellers no less often than those seeking to buy their wares are crooks. Another seller produced the documents quite quickly and with everything in place anyone could have been fooled. Not perhaps the e-passport gates at Heathrow, but a British passport is a gateway to many other forms of ID, as well as to a world of legitimacy. Slowly and digitally, "Ronnie" began to be a man who had everything, a face, an address, a passport, discount cards. He began to have conversations with real people on Reddit, or people who might have been real, and his Twitter and Facebook life showed him to be a creature of enthusiasm and prejudice. Nowadays, everyone can be Frankenstein and his monster, both the harebrained dreamer and his gothic offspring, and the enabling technology seems to encourage the idea. Ronnie, in the world, was a figment, but on discussion boards he was no less believable than anybody else. "Friend" has become a verb, leaving "befriend" to hint at the old world of warm handshakes and eyes that actually met. People "friend" people on Facebook and they get "friended," but many of them will never meet. Elsewhere on the Net the connections may lead to a cold presence, a person who is legitimate but nonexistent. Ronnie's social interaction online could be involved and energetic and characterful, but it seemed that everyone he met had a self to hide and nothing to show for themselves beyond their quips and departures. At one point, Ronnie's Twitter account got hacked and he was invaded by hundreds of robotic right-wing followers. His "information" had opened him up to being exploited by spambots, by other machines, and by Web detritus that clings to entities like Ronnie as a matter of digital course. None of these everyday spooks came in from the cold, and Ronnie moved, as if by osmosis, into the more criminal parts of the Internet, where the clandestine earns its keep.

It wasn't a million years ago that Marshall McLuhan was able to imagine the media as the benign source of a new togetherness: a place where "psychic communal integration" might occur. But our experience of the Internet is tangled with our sense of what its abusers are making of it. The technology is now a surveillance machine, a lying tool, a handheld marketing device, a corporate pinboard, a global platform for ideologues and zealots, as well as a handy life-enhancer. If Facebook, Twitter, Instagram, and the rest bring people together, they also complicate our notion of what a person is, and it's very different from former notions of reality and privacy. After several months, Ronnie had begun to press himself into some officially sanctioned world of paperwork, and, though the paperwork was false, his online demeanor suggested a reality as big as anyone's. The Ronald Pinn I created from the distant memory of a young man in a graveyard became, in imitation of the bent police officers who inspired his creation, an illegal alien in a world of bespoke reality. The police officers, under their new identities, had affairs and fathered children before disappearing home to their real lives and the world that squared with who they were. Ronnie Pinn had only one direction to go in, down and down into a world of seeming freedom, the Dark Web, where one can be anybody one wants to be, and at a happy advantage if "invented." The Dark Web is a place where rules can't be dictated by any external authority, a place that laughs at authority and authenticity. Normal search engines can't reach it and access can't easily be traced to anyone's computer. Ronnie found his natural domain in that world of few-questions-asked, though I was ready, by then, to answer any question about Ronnie that anyone might care to ask.

There was nothing obvious in the life of Ronnie that would have led directly to me or my own habits of invention, though I'd voiced him and played him. Once he had the means, the credentials, the bitcoins, and the passwords, he was, in a sense, free, like a character in fiction who must express himself not merely according to his author's wishes but according to some inner mechanisms embedded in his past and in his nature. "It begins with a character, usually," William Faulkner said, "and once he stands up on his feet and begins to move, all I can do is trot along behind him with paper and pencil trying to keep up long enough to put down what he says and does." And I can only say that the Ronald Pinn I made up tended toward certain enterprises of his own volition and I let him. The websites on the Dark Web have a tendency to morph as quickly as the people manning them, but the illicit marketplaces—Silk Road, Agora, Evolution—opened up to him, and he was soon having conversations with secretive experts about drugs and false documents and guns.

An individual called Ronald Pinn, using his own passcodes, paying with the bitcoins purchased in his name, bought white heroin and had it sent to his London address. It arrived in a small vacuum pack between two white cards in a Jiffy bag, and cost about thirty pounds. He bought Afghan weed and it came the same way; he bought Pakistani cannabis. Addressed to Ronald Pinn, it all came to the empty flat, and I had it checked for authenticity. At one point several packs of the powerful painkiller tramadol came through, as well as other drugs, all ordered by and delivered to the only person ever associated with their purchase, Ronald Pinn. As the weeks went by, his exploits became more baroque and seemed like a stretch for his character. He began buying counterfeit money, which came at 50 percent of the face value: for £200 you could buy £400 in fake money, and it passed all the basic tests. As an international space populated with anarchists and libertarians, nonconformists and government-haters, the Dark Web quite naturally gives itself to wide definitions of freedom. It points to the self-serving nature of power elites, decries corruption in governments and legal systems, satirizes the "phony" war on drugs, and laughs at all officialdom and all attempts to curtail the freedom of individuals. It likes drugs, has no respect for official banks, and has a fondness for guns.

Ronnie went in that direction. There were areas I wouldn't allow him to go into—porn, for instance—but the Ronnie who

THE INVENTION OF RONALD PINN   103

existed last summer was alive both to drugs and to the idea of
weaponry. It's one of the contradictions of the Dark Web, that its
love of throwing off constraints doesn't always sit well with its
live-and-let-live philosophy. There are people in those illicit
marketplaces who sell "suicide tablets" and bomb-making kits.
"Crowd-sourced hitmen" were on offer beside assault weapons,
bullets, and grenades. One of the odd things I discovered during
my time with cyberpurists—and Ronnie found it, too—was how
right-wing they are at the heart of their revolutionary programs.
The Internet is libertarian in spirit, as well as cultish, paranoid,
rabble-rousing, and demagogic, given to emptying other people's
trash cans while hiding its own, devoted not to persuasion but to
trolling, obsessed with making a religion of democracy while
broadly mistrusting people. Far down in the Dark Web, there
exists an antiauthoritarian madness, a love of disorder as long
as one's own possessions aren't threatened. The peaceniks come
holding grenades. The Manson Family would feel at home.

When Ronnie Pinn went to see this world he found it welcom-
ing and vile. He saw Uzis and assault rifles, bomb-making kits,
grenades, machetes, and pistols. As a man with cybercurrency,
he was welcome in every room and was never checked. He was
anybody as well as nobody. He could have been a teenager, a
warrior, a terrorist, or a psychopath. So long as he had currency
he was okay. The only two sites where the website operators
checked him out were Black Market Reloaded and Executive
Outcomes, both suppliers of weaponry. You could get past them,
but they did try to do checkups. Other sites on the Dark Web
asked no questions at all. Three hundred and fifteen grams of
brand-new gun with a nine-millimeter silencer? An AK-47 Black
Laminate, "with a chrome-lined central barrel, adjustable rear
sight and two 30-round magazines"? A Remington M-24 sniper
rifle? A series of Israeli-made semiautomatic pistols, costing less

than the retail price of $2,400? On the drugs discussion boards everyone seemed to be having the time of their life, but a sinister silence existed among the shootists. When a gun is purchased it arrives in many parts through the post, ready to be put together and used for who knows what purpose.

While Ronnie was becoming known in those circles, having chats, spending money, discovering what he and others could be and do, I was reaching back to see what more I could find out about the real Ronald Pinn. I stood one afternoon as an entire block of flats was being torn down on the Old Kent Road. I studied old photographs of Avondale Square and read through online chats where people remembered their childhood friends. I went to the former location of men's clothing shops, now pound shops; someone said the real Ronnie's family might have run businesses there. Nobody asked me why I was curious about this young man who died thirty years ago, as if it is normal to ask after people, as if that is just one of the things we do with our lives, asking after the dead. The cliché about reporting is that "ordinary" people don't want to have their lives invaded. But they do. More than anything they want to talk about who lived and who died and what changed. But who owns the narrative of a person's life? Do you own your own story? Do you own your children's? Or are these stories just part of what life manifested over the course of time, with no curator, no owner, no keeper who has the rights and holds the key? You have responsibilities and rights before the law, but do you own what you did and who you are, and is privacy a vain wish or an established right? Is there no copyright on one's experience and only the ability of others to remember or forget? I kept wondering about Ronnie's mother, whether she was alive somewhere. It seemed reasonable to expect that the story of Ronnie's real life would be something she felt she owned, or had to protect, and that the story of his second life would not only surprise her but feel like an invasion.

By the time I walked up the streets to his old schools, peered into the halls where he ate his school dinners and read his old report cards, the Ronnie Pinn who came after him, and used his birth certificate, was present and available to the mass consciousness of the World Wide Web and the Dark Web in ways that would have made the real Ronnie's mind boggle thirty years ago. It took three or four clicks to find the fake Ronnie and all his comments and many of the places he'd been. Before leaving my office to see the building where Ronald Pinn died in 1984, when I was sixteen, I looked into the possibility of buying the fake Ronnie a second passport, a Turkish one, and an "identity pack" (a bundle of fake ID cards and utility bills tailored to the buyer's chosen name and address, as well as their face). It was a busy morning. Using several bits of his fake ID, he got signed up for a gambling website. At his "address" in Islington I found that he now had a tax ID and was getting letters from the Inland Revenue. Was it only a matter of time before Ronnie was able to open a bank account, make investments, write his memoirs, and book a seat on a flight he would never arrive for?

With his fake self and his fake friends, Ronnie became like an ideal government "sleeper," a supposedly real person who could infiltrate political groups and shady markets. He started as a way of testing the Net's propensity to radicalize self-invention, but, by the end, I was controlling an entity with just enough of a basis in reality to reconfigure it. Ronnie Pinn's only handicap lay in his failure to materialize physically, but, nowadays, that needn't be a problem: everything he wanted to do, he could try to do, except find a partner, but even that, though tricky, was not impossible. I simply didn't go there for fear of fooling the innocent and learning nothing. He could chat people up online but when it came to meeting them, well, Ronnie was nothing, wasn't he? His existence was powerful in the dark and busy world of self-invention, but, like Peter Pan, he was a stranger to adulthood, and a grotesque outcrop of the imagination like Mr. Hyde; he lived for a season inside the mind of the person writing this story.

The "people" now moderating the Dark Web don't care about the old codes of citizenship and they don't recognize the laws of society. They don't believe that governments or currencies or historical narratives are automatically legitimate, or even that the personalities who appear to run the world are who they say they are. The average hacker believes most executives to be functionaries of a machine they can't understand. To the moderators of Silk Road or Agora, the world is an inchoate mass of desires and deceits, and everything that exists can be bought or sold, including selfhood, because to them freedom means stealing power back from the state, or God, or Apple, or Freud. To them, life is a drama in which power rubs out one's name; they are anonymous, ghosts in the machine, infiltrating and weakening the structures of the state and partying as they do so, causing havoc, encrypting who they are. When the FBI attacks Silk Road and attempts to shut it down, as it did in November 2014, the resilience it shows is impressive. "Our enemies may seize our servers," the moderators of Silk Road wrote on their relaunched website, "impound our coins, and arrest our friends, but they cannot stop you: our people. You write history with every coin transacted here . . . History will prove that we are not criminals, we are revolutionaries . . . Silk Road is not here to scam, we are here to end economic oppression. Silk Road is not here to promote violence, we are here to end the unjust war on drugs . . . Silk Road is not a marketplace. Silk Road is a global revolt." "When you're in a tsunami you can't push back the water," City of London Police

Commissioner Adrian Leppard said recently, when talking about piracy and the failure to hold it back. "You have to start thinking very differently about how we protect society . . . Enforcement will only ever be a limited capability in this space."

Ronnie Pinn, the invented one, was a single digit in "this space." He achieved all the legitimacy I could glean for him in the time I had. But always I was drawn back to the "real" Ronnie and what it meant to be out of the world for thirty years and then revived in a different guise. Eventually, I got a message from a woman I'd written to called Kathleen Pinn. In the first instance she said she thought Ronnie's mother might still be alive, and when I asked her to elaborate, she wrote again. "My family have never met up since my mother's death in 1979," she said. "Glenys was living in Bermondsey then, that's all I can tell you, I do not have her address." Eventually I found a number for her in a 1977 telephone directory, but the phone line was dead and the building was gone.

Eradicating the fake Ronnie was difficult. He had sixty-eight followers on Twitter and I don't suppose many of them noticed he'd gone; some of them were as fake as he was. But rubbing out a Twitter account leaves a shadow on the Net. It used to be that real people could go missing and nobody would really notice, and nothing would be left behind. Life used to be good at that. But nowadays the fake identities are hard to abolish, and something of the fake Ronnie is indelible, his "legend" part of the general ether. He has "metadata," the stuff that governments collect, the chaff of being. And he will go on existing in that universe though he never existed on earth.

Ronnie's last tweet was a single word, "Goodbye," on December 12, 2014; then I deleted his account. "We will retain your user data for 30 days," Twitter told me, but "we have no control over content indexed by search engines like Google." His unreality was now embedded in the system; it would never have to explain itself. On Facebook, there was a final "friend" request from someone called Peter Lux: I have no idea who Mr. Lux is, or why he wanted to friend Ronnie Pinn, or if he is even real or just another figment shoring up his legend. Facebook doesn't make it easy to deactivate an account: it wants you to stay. "Laura will miss you," the message said, choosing one of Ronnie's "friends" at random. And then: "Your 23 friends will no longer be able to keep in touch with you," before warning me that "messages you sent may still be available on friends' accounts." When it let me leave, it demanded that I tick a box saying why I was leaving and I chose one that seemed right: "I have a privacy concern." Reddit was also sorry to see Ronnie Pinn go, and his conversations, about freedom, about guns, about drugs, would never necessarily be wiped and would remain up there like a dead star.

Ronnie's online gambling account, which was set up using false documents, couldn't be closed down. Craigslist promised his account would self-delete after a few months of inactivity. The bitcoins laundering service, a secret service alert to the very last, had no record of Ronnie buying anything and his "presence" disappeared as soon as I deleted his e-mail accounts and ripped up the passwords. "We're sorry to see you leave!" Gmail said, but the we that was sorry was never identified, and traces of who Ronnie was and what he did through various e-mail accounts are now hidden in servers around the world. My invention had become so present in the official world of things that as well as a tax ID he had a national insurance number, though I had never tried to register Ronnie as a taxpayer or as someone drawing a salary. Banks were soliciting his custom, and though he wasn't on the electoral roll, it seemed only a matter of time. The flat in Islington had nothing to do with Ronnie and no one who lived in the building had ever heard of him, though it felt strange when I went to the hall for the last time and picked up his letters.

I'd almost given up when I found Ronnie's mother. Her name was on a register I had in my possession all along, and it seemed to prove she was still alive. There was no phone number, and the house was to the northeast of London, almost in Essex. I held on to the details for a few weeks more, putting a card on my desk with the address written on it. Every morning I looked at it and wondered if solid reality wouldn't yet prove something more. Then, one morning at the end of November while it was still dark outside, I got up and got dressed, put my recorder and a notebook in my bag, and walked out into the rain. The Tube was crowded at Bank, everyone keeping themselves to themselves, the Indian lady in sandals and socks, the young man with earphones and jagged hair lost in beats not his own; the lady across from me with the Aztec necklace, the man in the North Face jacket, the schoolchild looking out anxiously for her stop. All the while I was thinking about Mrs. Pinn. Would she be out of bed now, making tea and wondering what the day would hold? Would she be pulling back the curtains, coming down the stairs, not knowing that today was the day a stranger would come to speak to her about her son? I thought about her as the train stretched away beyond Central London and the commuters left group by group until, past Barkingside, there was only me. The morning's newspapers were blowing down the carriage, and it grew light over the fields.

I walked for a mile or so to find the house. I wasn't sure it would be the right one, or that the Mrs. Pinn I'd find there was the person I was looking for. There was a strong chance she wouldn't want to speak to me and would hate the whole thing. I knew all that, and the streetlamps blinked off as I walked under an overpass and past a bank of skinny trees. An elderly man stood behind a hedge at the end of Mrs. Pinn's street. The path was neat as I walked up to the house, and the garden was simple. There was a dog barking inside and I stood for a moment. An elderly, good-looking woman came to the kitchen window and we each stared for a moment. She was wearing a leopard-pattern dressing gown and holding the dog's tiny yellow ball. She opened the kitchen window expecting a salesman and was surprised when I said her name. I said I wanted to speak to her about Ronnie and I would explain everything. Her eyes widened and she seemed astonished for a second as she said the word "Ronnie." I noticed she squeezed the yellow ball before nodding and coming to the door. "It will be nice to talk to you," she said, letting me into the hall. "You must be about his age."

"That's right."

"Oh, Ronnie," she said. "There was nobody like him."

The Satoshi Affair

The Raid

Ten men raided a house in Gordon, a north shore suburb of Sydney, at 1:30 p.m. on Wednesday, December 9, 2015. Some of the federal agents wore shirts that said "Computer Forensics"; one carried a search warrant issued under the Australian Crimes Act 1914. They were looking for a man named Craig Steven Wright, who lived with his wife, Ramona, at 43 St. Johns Avenue. The warrant was issued at the behest of the Australian Taxation Office (ATO). Wright, a computer scientist and businessman, headed a group of companies associated with cryptocurrency and online security. Wright and his wife were gone but the agents entered the house by force. As one set of agents scoured his kitchen cupboards and emptied out his garage, another entered his main company headquarters at 32 Delhi Road in North Ryde, another suburb of Sydney. They were looking for "originals or copies" of material held on hard drives and computers; they wanted bank statements, mobile-phone records, research papers, and photographs. The warrant listed dozens of companies whose papers were to be scrutinized, and thirty-two individuals, some with alternative names, or alternative spellings. The name Satoshi Nakamoto appeared sixth from the bottom of the list.

Some of the Wrights' neighbors at St. Johns Avenue say they were a little distant. She was friendly but he was weird—to one neighbor he was "Cold-Shoulder Craig"—and their landlord wondered why they needed so much extra power: Wright had what appeared to be a whole room full of generators at the back of the property. This fed a rack of computers that he called his "toys," but the real computer, on which he'd spent a lot of money, was nearly nine thousand miles away in Panama. He had already taken the computers away the day before the raid. A reporter had turned up at the house and Wright, alarmed, had phoned Stefan, the man advising them on what he and Ramona were calling "the deal." Stefan immediately moved Wright and his wife into a luxury apartment at the Meriton World Tower in Sydney. They'd soon be moving to England anyway, and all parties agreed it was best to hide out for now.

At 32 Delhi Road, the palm trees were throwing summer shade onto the concrete walkways—"Tailor Made Office Solutions," it said on a nearby billboard—and people were drinking coffee in Deli 32 on the ground floor. Wright's office on level five was painted red, and looked down on the Macquarie Park Cemetery, known as a place of calm for the living as much as for the dead. No one was sure what to do when the police entered. The staff were gathered in the middle of the room and told by the officers not to go near their computers or use their phones. "I tried to intervene," one senior staff member, a Dane called Allan Pedersen, remarked later, "and said we would have to call our lawyers."

Holed up in the Meriton World Tower, Ramona wasn't keen to tell her family what was happening. The reporters were sniffing at a strange story—a story too complicated for her to explain—so she just told everyone that damp in the Gordon house had forced them to move out. The place they moved into, a tall apartment building, was right in the city and Wright felt as if he was on holiday. On December 9, after their first night in the new apartment, he woke up to the news that two articles, one on the technology site *Gizmodo*, the other in the tech magazine *Wired*, had come out overnight fingering him as the person behind the pseudonym Satoshi Nakamoto, who in 2008 published a white paper describing a "peer-to-peer electronic cash system"—a technology Satoshi went on to develop as bitcoin. Reading the articles on his laptop, Wright knew his old life was over.

By this point, cameras and reporters were outside his former home and his office. They had long heard rumors, but the *Gizmodo* and *Wired* stories had sent the Australian media into a frenzy. It wasn't clear why the police and the articles had appeared on the same day. At about five that same afternoon, a receptionist called from the lobby of Wright's apartment building to say that the police had arrived. Ramona turned to Wright and told him to get the hell out. He looked at a desk in front of the window: there were two large laptop computers on it—they weighed a few kilos each, with 64 gigabytes of RAM—and he grabbed the one that wasn't yet fully encrypted. He also took Ramona's phone, which wasn't encrypted either, and headed for the door. They were on the sixty-third floor. It occurred to him that the police might be coming up in the elevator, so he went down to the sixty-first floor, where there were office suites and a swimming pool. He stood frozen for a minute before he realized he'd rushed out without his passport.

Ramona left the apartment shortly after Wright. She went straight down to the basement car park and was relieved to find the police weren't guarding the exits. She jumped into her car, a hire vehicle, and, in her panic, crashed into the exit barrier. But she didn't stop, and was soon on the freeway heading to north Sydney. She just wanted to be somewhere familiar where she would have time to think. She felt vulnerable without her phone, and decided to drive to a friend's and borrow his. She went to his workplace and took his phone, telling him she couldn't explain because she didn't want to get him involved.

Meanwhile, Wright was still standing beside the swimming pool in his suit, with a laptop in his arms. He heard people coming up the stairs, sped down the corridor, and ducked into the gents'. A bunch of teenagers were standing around but seemed not to notice him. He went to the farthest cubicle and deliberately kept the door unlocked. (He figured the police would just look for an ENGAGED sign.) He was standing on top of the toilet when he heard the officers come in. They asked the youngsters what they were doing, but they said "nothing" and the police left. Wright stayed in the cubicle for a few minutes, then went out and used his apartment keycard to hide in the service stairwell. Eventually, a call came from Ramona on her friend's phone. She was slightly horrified to discover he was still in the building and told him again to get out. He, too, had a rental car, and had the key in his pocket. He went down sixty flights of stairs to the parking lot in the basement, unlocked his car, and opened the trunk, where he lifted out the spare wheel and put his laptop in the wheel cavity. He drove toward the Harbour Bridge and got lost in the traffic.

As Ramona drove along she began texting the mysterious Stefan, who was at Sydney Airport, having already checked in for a flight to Manila, where he lived. Stefan had to make a fuss to get his bag removed from the plane. He then headed back into Sydney and he spoke en route to Ramona, telling her that Wright would have to get out of the country. She didn't argue. She called the Flight Centre and asked what flights were leaving. "To where?" asked the saleswoman.

THE SATOSHI AFFAIR   117

"Anywhere," Ramona said. Within ten minutes she had booked her husband on a flight to Auckland.

In the early evening, Wright, scared and lost, made his way to the shopping district of Chatswood, an area he knew well and in which he felt comfortable. He texted Ramona to come and meet him, and she immediately texted back saying he should go straight to the airport; she'd booked him a flight. "But I don't have my passport," he said. Ramona was afraid she'd be arrested if she returned to their apartment, but her friend said he'd go into the building and get the passport. They waited until the police left the building, then he went upstairs. A few minutes later he came back with the passport, along with the other computer and a power supply.

They met Wright in the airport parking lot. Ramona had never seen him so worried. "I was shocked," he later said. "I hadn't expected to be outed like that in the media, and then to be chased down by the police. Normally, I'd be prepared. I'd have a bag packed." As Ramona gave him the one-way ticket to Auckland, she was anxious about when she would see him again. Wright said New Zealand was a bit too close and wondered what to do about money. Ramona went to an ATM and gave him six hundred dollars. He bought a yellow bag from the airport shop in which to store his computers. He had no clothes. "It was awful saying goodbye to him," Ramona said.

In the queue for security, he felt nervous about his computers. His flight was about to close when the security staff flagged him down. He was being taken to an interview room when an Indian man behind him started going berserk. It was just after the Paris bombings; the man's wife was wearing a sari and the security staff wanted to pat her down. The man objected. All the security staff ran over to deal with the situation and Wright was told to go. He couldn't believe his luck. He put his head down and scurried through the lounge.

Back at Wright's office, Allan Pedersen was being interviewed by the police. He overheard one of them ask: "Have we got Wright yet?"

"He's just hopped a flight to New Zealand," his colleague said.

Wright was soon 30,000 feet above the Tasman Sea watching the programmer Thomas Anderson (Keanu Reeves) being chased by unknowable agents in *The Matrix*. Wright found the story line strangely comforting; it was good to know he wasn't alone.

At Auckland Airport, Wright kept his phone on flight mode but turned it on to Skype with Stefan using the airport's Wi-Fi and a new account. They had a discussion about how to get him to Manila. There was a big rock concert that night in Auckland, and all the hotels were full, but he crossed town in a cab and managed to get a small room at the Hilton. He booked two nights, using cash. He knew how to get more cash out of ATMs than the daily limit, so he worked several machines near the hotel, withdrawing five thousand dollars. He ordered room service that night and the next morning went to the Billabong store in Queen Street to buy some clothes. He felt agitated, out of his element: normally he would wear a suit and tie—he enjoys the notion that he is too well-dressed to be a geek—but he bought a T-shirt, a pair of jeans, and some socks. On the way back to the hotel he got a bunch of SIM cards, so that his calls wouldn't be monitored. Back at the Hilton he was packing up his computers when the dependable Stefan came on Skype. He told Wright to go to the airport and pick up a ticket he'd left him for a flight to Manila. His picture was all over the papers, along with the story that he was trying to escape.

Within hours of Wright's name appearing in the press, anonymous messages threatened to reveal his "actual history." Some said he had been on Ashley Madison, the website that sets up extramarital affairs, others that he'd been seen on Grindr, the gay hookup app. During a six-hour layover in Hong Kong, he killed his e-mail accounts and tried to wipe his social media profile, which he knew would be heavy with information he wasn't keen to publicize: "Mainly rants," he said later. When he got to Manila airport, Stefan picked him up. They went to Stefan's apartment and the maid washed Wright's clothes while he set up his laptops on the dining room table. They spent the rest of Saturday wiping his remaining social media profile. Stefan didn't want any contact to be possible: he wanted to cut Wright off from the world. The next day he put him on a plane to London.

Mayfair

Technology is constantly changing the lives of people who don't really understand it—we drive our cars, and care nothing for internal combustion—but now and then a story will break that captures the imagination of the general public. I was one of the people who had never heard of Satoshi Nakamoto or the blockchain—the invention underlying bitcoin, which verifies transactions without the need for any central authority—or that it is the biggest thing in computer science. It was news to me that the banks were grabbing on to the blockchain as the foundation of a future "Internet of value." If it hadn't been for my involvement with Assange, the story of this mythical computer scientist might never have come my way. I'm not much detained by thoughts of new computer paradigms. (I'm still getting the hang of the first one.) But to those who are much more invested in the world of tomorrow, the Satoshi story has the lineaments of a modern morality tale quite independent of stock realities. There

are things, there are always things, that others assume are at the
center of the universe but don't make a scratch on your own
sense of the everyday world. This story was like that for me, enclosing me in an enigma I couldn't have named. A long-form
report is a fashioned thing, of course, as fashioned as fiction in
its own ways, but I had to overcome my own bafflement—as will
you—to enter this world.

A few weeks before the raid on Craig Wright's house, when
his name still hadn't ever been publicly associated with Satoshi
Nakamoto, I got an e-mail from a Los Angeles lawyer called Jimmy
Nguyen, from the firm Davis Wright Tremaine (self-described as
"a one-stop shop for companies in entertainment, technology,
advertising, sports and other industries"). Nguyen told me that
they were looking to contract me to write the life of Satoshi
Nakamoto. "My client has acquired life story rights . . . from the
true person behind the pseudonym Satoshi Nakamoto—the creator of the bitcoin protocol," the lawyer wrote. "The story will be
[of] great interest to the public and we expect the book project will
generate significant publicity and media coverage once Satoshi's
true identity is revealed."

Journalists, it turned out, had spent years looking for Nakamoto. His identity was one of the great mysteries of the Internet,
and a holy grail of investigative reporting, with writers who
couldn't dig up evidence simply growing their own. For *The New
Yorker*'s Joshua Davis the need to find him seemed almost pain-
ful. "Nakamoto himself was a cipher," he wrote in October 2011:

> Before the debut of bitcoin, there was no record of any coder
> with that name. He used an e-mail address and a Web site that
> were untraceable. In 2009 and 2010, he wrote hundreds of posts
> in flawless English, and though he invited other software devel-
> opers to help him improve the code, and corresponded with

them, he never revealed a personal detail. Then, in April, 2011, he sent a note to a developer saying that he had "moved on to other things." He has not been heard from since.

Davis went on to examine Satoshi's writing quite closely and concluded that he used British spelling and was fond of the word "bloody." He then named a twenty-three-year-old Trinity College Dublin graduate student, Michael Clear, who quickly denied it. The story went nowhere and Clear went back to his studies. Then Leah McGrath Goodman wrote a piece for *Newsweek* claiming Satoshi was a math genius called Dorian Nakamoto, who lived in the Los Angeles suburb of Temple City and didn't actually know, it turned out, how to pronounce "bitcoin." When Goodman's article ran on the magazine's cover, reporters from all over the world arrived on Dorian's doorstep. He said he would give an interview to the first person who would take him to lunch. It turned out that his hobby wasn't alternative currencies but model trains. Someone calling himself Satoshi Nakamoto, and using Satoshi's original e-mail address, visited one of the forums Satoshi used to haunt and posted the message "I am not Dorian Nakamoto." Other commentators, including Nathaniel Popper of *The New York Times*, named Nick Szabo, a cool cryptocurrency nut and the inventor of digital money called Bit Gold, but he denied it profusely. *Forbes* believed it was Hal Finney, who, the blockchain irrefutably showed, was the first person in the world to be sent bitcoins by Satoshi. Finney, a native Californian, was an expert cryptographer whose involvement in the development of bitcoin was vital. He was diagnosed with motor neuron disease in 2009 and died in 2014. It came to seem that the holy grail would remain out of reach. "Many in the bitcoin community . . . in deference to the bitcoin creator's clear desire for privacy . . . didn't want to see the wizard unmasked," Popper wrote in *The*

New York Times. "But even among those who said this, few could resist debating the clues the founder left behind."

As with every story I've ever worked on, I checked the background and made a number of calls before I got back to the lawyers representing the mysterious client. The client's idea, I then discovered from the lawyers, was that I would have full access to their man, Satoshi, to write a book and have it published as I saw fit. I listened carefully and I took some advice; I wanted to be careful. I had to find out exactly what these clients were looking for and why they'd come to me. This information came slowly, and I let the deal remain vague, I signed nothing, while I worked out who they were. The "Stefan" who was hovering during the raid on Craig Wright's house and office is Stefan Matthews, an Australian IT expert whom Wright had known for ten years, since they both worked for the online gambling site Centrebet. In those days, around 2007, Wright was often hired as a security analyst by such firms, deploying his skills as a computer scientist (and his experience as a hacker) to make life difficult for fraudsters. Wright was an eccentric guy, Stefan Matthews remembered, but known to be a reliable freelancer. Matthews told me that Wright had given him a document to look at in 2008 written by someone called Satoshi Nakamoto, but Matthews had been busy at the time and didn't read it for a while. He said that Wright was always trying to get him interested in this new venture called bitcoin. He tried to sell him 50,000 bitcoins for next to nothing, but Matthews wasn't interested, he told me, because Wright was weird and the whole thing seemed a bit cranky. A few years later, however, Matthews realized that the document he had been shown was, in fact, an original draft of the by-now-famous white paper by Satoshi Nakamoto. (Like the governments they despise, bitcoiners deal—when it comes to ideas—in "white papers," as if they are issuing laws.)

In 2015, when Wright was in financial trouble—his companies were facing bankruptcy and he was at the end of his wits—he approached Matthews several times. By then, Matthews had become friendly with Robert MacGregor, the founder and CEO of a Canada-based money-transfer firm called nTrust. Matthews encouraged MacGregor to come to Australia and assess Wright's value as an investment opportunity. Wright had founded a number of businesses that were failing and he was deeply embedded in a dispute with the ATO. Nevertheless, Matthews told MacGregor, Wright was almost certainly the man behind bitcoin.

Matthews argued that since Satoshi's disappearance in 2011, Wright had been working on new applications of the blockchain technology he had invented as Satoshi. He was, in other words, using the technology underlying bitcoin to create new versions of the formula that could, at a stroke, replace the systems of bookkeeping and registration and centralized authority that banks and governments depend on. Wright and his people were preparing dozens of patents, and each invention, in a specific way, looked to rework financial, social, legal, or medical services, expanding on the basic idea of the "distributed public ledger" that constitutes the blockchain. The math behind the technology can be mind-boggling, but bitcoin is a form of digital money where the flow and the integrity of the currency are guaranteed by its appearance on a shared public ledger, updated and refreshed with every single transaction, a "public history" that cannot be corrupted by any single entity. It works by consensus, and is secured by a series of private and public encryption keys. It is like a Google document that can be used and updated by anyone linked into the "chain." The blockchain can do many things, but the revolutionary aspect is that it takes authoritarianism and sharp practice out of the banking system, embedding all power over the currency within the self-cleansing software itself and the people who use it. Blockchain technology is a hot topic in computer science and banking at the moment, and hundreds of millions of dollars are being invested in such ideas. Thus: Matthews's proposal.

MacGregor came out to Australia in May 2015. After initial skepticism, and in spite of a slight aversion to Wright's manner, he was persuaded, and struck a deal with Wright, signed on June 29, 2015. MacGregor says he felt sure that Wright was bitcoin's legendary missing father, and he told me it was his idea, later in the drafting of the deal, to insist that Satoshi's "life rights" be included as part of the agreement. Wright's companies were so deep in debt that the deal appeared to him like a rescue plan, so he agreed to everything, without, it seems, really examining what he would have to do. Within a few months, according to evidence later given to me by Matthews and MacGregor, the deal would cost MacGregor's company $15 million. "That's right," Matthews said to me in February 2016. "When we signed the deal, 1.5 million dollars was given to Wright's lawyers. But my main job was to set up an engagement with the new lawyers . . . and transfer Wright's intellectual property to nCrypt"—a newly formed subsidiary of nTrust. "The deal had the following components: clear the outstanding debts that were preventing Wright's business from getting back on its feet, and work with the new lawyers on getting the agreements in place for the transfer of any noncorporate intellectual property, and work with the lawyers to get Craig's story rights." From that point on, the "Satoshi revelation" would be part of the deal. "It was the cornerstone of the commercialization plan," Matthews said, "with about ten million sunk into the Australian debts and setting up in London."

The plan was always clear to the men behind nCrypt. They would bring Wright to London and set up a research and development center for him, with around thirty staff working under him. They would complete the work on his inventions and patent applications—he appeared to have hundreds of them—and the whole lot would be sold as the work of Satoshi Nakamoto, who would be unmasked as part of the project. Once packaged, Matthews and MacGregor planned to sell the intellectual property for upward of a billion dollars. MacGregor later told me he was speaking to Google and Uber, as well as to a number of Swiss banks. "The plan was to package it all up and sell it," Matthews told me. "The plan was never to operate it."

Since the time I worked with Julian Assange, my computers have been hacked several times. It isn't unusual for me to find that material has been wiped—at one point 30,000 e-mails—and I was careful to make sure the Los Angeles lawyers' approach wasn't part of a sting operation. Not long after their initial approach, the lawyers had mentioned that the company behind the deal was called nTrust. I did some research and the lawyers then confirmed that the "client" referred to in the initial e-mail was Robert MacGregor. I was soon in correspondence with MacGregor himself. On Thursday, November 12, I turned up, by appointment, at his office near Oxford Circus, where I signed in under a pseudonym and made my way to a boardroom wallpapered with mathematical formulae. MacGregor came into the room wearing a tailored jacket and jeans, with a blue-edged pocket square in his breast pocket, a scarf, and brown brogue boots. He was forty-seven but looked about twenty-nine. There was something studied about him—the Alexander McQueen scarf, the lawyerly punctilio—and I'd never met anyone who spoke so easily about such large sums of money. When I asked him the point of the whole exercise, he said it was simple: "Buy in, sell out, make some zeroes."

MacGregor described Wright to me as "the goose that lays the golden egg." He said that if I agreed to take part I would have exclusive access to the whole story, and to everyone around Wright, and that it would all end with Wright proving he was Satoshi by using cryptographic keys that only Satoshi had access to, those associated with the very first blocks in the blockchain. MacGregor told me this might happen at a public TED talk. He said it would be "game over." Wright's patents would then be sold and Wright could get on with his life, out of the public eye. "All he wants is peace to get on with his work," MacGregor told me at that first meeting. "And how this ends, for me, is with Craig working for, say, Google, with a research staff of four hundred."

I told MacGregor that there would have to be a process of verification. We talked about money, and negotiated a little, but after several meetings I decided I wouldn't accept any. I would write the story as I had every other story under my name, by observing and interviewing, taking notes and making recordings, and sifting the evidence. "It should be warts and all," MacGregor said. He said it several times, but I was never sure he understood what it meant. This was a changing story, and I was the only one keeping account of the changes. MacGregor and his coworkers were already convinced Wright was Satoshi, and they behaved, to my mind, as if that claim was the end of the story, rather than the beginning.

I don't mean to imply anything sinister. The company was excited by the project and so was I. Very quickly we were working hand in hand: I reserved judgment (and independence) but I was caught up in the thought of the story unfolding as planned. At this point, nobody knew who Craig Wright was, but he appeared, from the initial evidence, to have a better claim to being

Satoshi Nakamoto than anyone else had. He seemed to have the technical ability. He also had the right social history, and the timeline worked. The big proof was up ahead, and how could it not be spectacular? I went slowly forward with the project, and said no to everything that would hamper my independence. This would become an issue later on with MacGregor and Matthews, or the men in black, as I'd taken to calling them, but for those first few months, nobody asked me to sign anything and nobody refused me access. Mysteries would open up, and some would remain, but there seemed no mystery about the fact that these people were confident that a supremely important thing was happening and that the entire process should be witnessed and recorded. My e-mails to MacGregor took it for granted that what would be good for my story, in terms of securing proof, would also be good for his deal, and that seemed perfectly true. Yet I feel bad that I didn't warn him of the possibility that this might not be what happened, that my story wouldn't die if the deal died, that human interest doesn't stop at success.

It was at this point, four weeks after my first meeting with MacGregor, that *Wired* and *Gizmodo* reported that Wright might be Satoshi. The news unleashed a tsunami of responses from the cryptocurrency community, and most of it was bad for Wright's credibility. Had he left artificial footprints to suggest his involvement with bitcoin had been earlier than it was? Had he exaggerated the number and nature of the degrees he'd accumulated from various universities? Why did the company that supplied the supercomputer he claimed to have bought with amassed bitcoin say it had never heard of him?

"The smell," as one commentator said, "was a mile high." The nCrypt people were unfazed by this mudslinging, believing that every one of the charges made against Wright could be easily disproved. Wright produced an impressive paper—for internal use only—showing that his "footprint" wasn't faked and that the "cryptographic" evidence against him was bogus (people continue to argue on this point). The accusation of fraud didn't seem to bother the nCrypt people. I was a bit confused by the mudslinging, but I kept listening. Wright produced a letter from the supercomputer supplier acknowledging the order. Charles Sturt University provided a photocopy of his staff card, proving he had lectured there, and Wright sent me a copy of the thesis he'd submitted for a doctorate his critics claim he doesn't have.

I had arrived five minutes early at 28°–50°, a wine bar and restaurant in Mayfair. It was just before 1 p.m. on December 16 and the lunchtime crowd, men in blue suits and white shirts, were eating oysters and baby back ribs and drinking high-end wine by the glass. A jeroboam of Graham's ten-year-old tawny port stood on the bar, and I was inspecting it when MacGregor arrived with Mr. and Mrs. Smith. That's what he'd been calling them in his e-mails to me. Craig Wright, forty-five years old, wearing a white shirt under a black jacket, a pair of blue chinos, a belt with a large Armani buckle, and very green socks, wasn't the kind of guy who seems comfortable in a swish restaurant. He sat across from me and lowered his head and at first he let MacGregor do the talking. Ramona was very friendly, chatting about their time in London as if they were a couple of holidaymakers who'd just blown into Mayfair. She wasn't drinking, but the rest of us ordered a glass of Malbec each. When Wright lifted his head to laugh at something, I noticed he had a nice smile but uneven teeth, and a scar that climbed from the top of his nose to the area just above his left eyebrow. He hadn't shaved for a week, since he'd left Sydney.

Wright told me he was rubbish at small talk. He, too, wanted what I wrote to be "warts and all"; he felt he was being misunderstood by everybody, and normally that wouldn't bother him but he had to consider the respectability of his work, and his family's rights. He appeared to ponder this for a moment, then he told me his old neighbors at the house in Gordon hadn't been friendly.

"They barely even knew your name," Ramona said.

"They do now," he replied.

I found him easier to talk to than I'd expected. He said his father had worked for the NSA (he could provide no further information), but that, to this day, his mother thinks he worked for NASA. "The few people I care about I care about a lot," he said, "and I care about the state of the world. But there's not much in between." He said he was happy I was writing about him because he wanted "to step into history," but mainly because he wanted to tell the story of the brilliant people he had collaborated with. He and Ramona were both jet-lagged and anxious about things back home. "We should have been having our company's Christmas party today," Ramona said.

MacGregor asked Wright if being a libertarian had influenced his work, or if the work had turned him into a libertarian. "I was always libertarian," he replied, and then he told me his father had more or less kidnapped him after his parents got divorced. He hated being told what to do—that was one of his main motivations. He believed in freedom, and in what freedom would come to mean, and he said his work would guarantee a future in which privacy was protected. "Where we are," he said, "is a place where people can be private and part of that privacy is to be someone other than who they were. Computing will allow you to start again, if you want to. And that is freedom." In fact he never stopped imagining different lives for himself. That afternoon he seemed preoccupied by the case people were making against his being Satoshi. He shook his head a lot and said he wished he could just get on in silence with his work. "If you want to stay sane through this, ignore Reddit," his wife told him.

The next day, December 17, we met again, in a private room in Claridge's. You could see outside, over the rooftops, cranes garlanded in fairy lights. Ramona came in looking tired and totally fed up. From time to time, especially when exhausted, she would resent the hold these people had over them. "We have sold our souls," she said to me in a quiet moment.

MacGregor said he would spend the evening preparing paperwork to be signed by Wright the following day. This would effectively be the final signing over to nCrypt of the intellectual property held by Wright's companies. This was the main plank in the deal. MacGregor was confident the work was "world historical," that it would change the way we lived. He regularly described the blockchain as the greatest invention since the Internet. He said that what the Internet had done for communication, the blockchain would do for value.

MacGregor explained that Wright's Australian companies were being signed over to nCrypt and that he'd extended an "olive branch" to the ATO, which had responded quickly and positively. A lot of trouble with the ATO had to do with whether bitcoin was a commodity or a currency and how it should be taxed. It also had doubts about whether Wright's companies had done as much research and development as they claimed, and whether they were therefore entitled to the tax rebates they had applied for. The ATO had said it couldn't see where the spending was going. Some critics in the media claimed Wright's companies had been set up only for the purpose of claiming rebates, though not even the ATO went that far.

Wright told me that thanks to the tax office they'd had to lay out all the research for their patents, which had been useful since the nCrypt team was in a hurry: the banks, now alert to cryptocurrencies and the effectiveness of the blockchain, are rushing to create their own versions. At that moment, Bank of America was patenting ten ideas for which Craig and his team told me they had a claim to "prior art." Governments spent a long time denying the value of bitcoin—seeing it as unstable, or the currency of criminals—but now they were celebrating the potential of the technology behind it.

"They're behaving like children," Wright said of the ATO.

MacGregor looked at his watch. He straightened his cuffs. "I see this as a pivotal moment in history . . . It's like being able to go back in time and watch Bill Gates in the garage." He turned to Wright. "You released this thing into the wild. Some people got it right and some people got it wrong. But you've got a vision of where it's going next and next and next."

"None of this would have worked without bitcoin," Wright said, "but it's a wheel and I want to build a car."

Ramona looked depressed. She was worried that her husband, as the person claiming to have invented bitcoin, might be held liable for the actions of those who'd used the currency for nefarious purposes. "He didn't issue a currency," MacGregor assured her. "This is just technology—it is not money." Ramona was still anxious. "We're talking about legal risk . . . I'm giving you the legal answer," MacGregor said. "I would stake my career on the fact that the creation of bitcoin is not a prosecutable event."

Right to the end, the Wrights would express worries about things Craig did as a young computer forensics worker. Much of his professional past looked questionable, but in the meeting room at Claridge's he simply batted the past away. "It's what you're doing now that matters. I'm not perfect. I never will be . . . All these different people arguing about what Satoshi should be at the moment, it's crazy."

Ninjutsu

Wright's father, Frederick Page Wright, was a forward scout in Vietnam, serving with the 8th Battalion of the Australian Army. "He lost all his friends," Wright told me, "every single one of them"—and before long he was drinking and being violent toward Wright's mother, who eventually left him. Both Wright and his mother, when I went to meet her in Brisbane in March 2016, told me about his father's anger at his own mother: he sent all his army paychecks home to her and she spent them while he was away. He also dreamed of a soccer career that never happened. "I have a chip on my shoulder," Wright said, "but his was bigger."

"Did you admire him?"

"He never admired me. I was never fucking good enough. We played chess from when I was three or four and if I made a wrong move he'd wallop me. We clashed right from the beginning."

The boy had two great influences. The first was his grandfather Ronald Lyman, who his family claims received the first degree awarded by the Marconi School of Wireless in Australia, and who served in the army as a signals officer. They also say he later became a spy with the Australian security services. Craig's favorite place was his grandfather's basement, a paradise of early computing. "We'd sit there and look at these books of log tables," he told me. "I loved doing it." Captain Lyman had an old terminal and a Hayes 80-103A modem that they used to connect to the University of Melbourne's network. To keep Craig quiet while he worked, Pop, as the children called him, would let him write code. "I found this community of hackers," Wright says, "and I worked out how to interact with them. I started building games and hacking other people's games. In time, I'd be pulling apart hacker code, and eventually I did this for companies, to help them create defenses against hackers."

His mother told me he was sometimes picked on at school. "He struggled," she said, "but after a while I sent him to Padua College"—a private Catholic academy in Brisbane—"and he shone there. I mean, he was different. He used to dress up and he had an obsession with Japanese culture. He had big samurai swords."

"As a teenager?"

"Dressed up in samurai clothes, with the odd wooden shoes and everything. Making all the noises. His sisters would complain about him embarrassing them: 'We're down the park, we've got friends down there, and he's walking around with webbed feet.' He used to have this group of nerdy friends in the 1980s: they'd come around in horn-rimmed glasses and play Dungeons and Dragons for hours."

He had a karate teacher called Mas who moved him quickly from karate through judo to ninjutsu. Craig broke his knuckles over and over again and "became stronger," he told me, because "the pain led to a 'me' that could handle more." The thing that attracted him most to martial arts was the discipline. Learning to become a ninja involves eighteen disciplines, including *bōjutsu* (tactics), *hensōjutsu* (disguise and impersonation), *intonjutsu* (escape and concealment), and *shinobi-iri* (stealth and infiltration). He walked home from his lessons feeling stronger, like another self.

When he was eighteen, Wright joined the air force. "They locked me in a bunker," he told me, "and I worked on a bombing system. Smart bombs. We needed fast code, and I did that." When he was in his twenties a melanoma appeared on his back and he had several skin grafts. "This was after he got out of the air force," his mother told me, "and when he recovered he was off to university, and it's been degrees, degrees, degrees since then." He went to the University of Queensland to study computer systems engineering. And over the following twenty-five years he would finish, or not finish, or finish and not do the graduation paperwork for degrees in digital forensics, nuclear physics, theology, management, network security, international commercial law, and statistics. After our first full interview, he went home to work on an assignment for a new course he was taking at the University of London, a masters in quantitative finance.

Over the months I spent with him, I noticed that he loved the idea of heroism and was strongly attracted to creation myths. One of the first things he e-mailed me was a copy of one of his dissertations, "Gnarled Roots of a Creation Mythos." I noticed it was dedicated to Mas, his martial arts instructor. The text wasn't merely an argument for self-invention, but a feminist exegesis that railed against patriarchal views of the Fall. Wright also speaks of the pilgrim-visitor in the "world garden": "While in the garden, the pilgrim almost inevitably suffers deception. His or her senses, enchanted by illusory and transitory formal appearances, betray his or her soul and lead to sin."

Wright said he had never expected the myth of Satoshi to gather such force. "We were all used to using pseudonyms," he told me. "That's the cypherpunk way. Now people want Satoshi to come down from the mountain like a messiah. I am not *that*. And we didn't mean to set up a myth that way." Satoshi was loved by bitcoin fans for making a beautiful thing and then disappearing. They don't want Satoshi to be wrong or contradictory, boastful or short-tempered, and they really don't want him to be a forty-five-year-old Australian called Craig.

While reading Wright's ideas on creation, I kept thinking of his karate teacher and the position he had in the young man's life. An offhand remark Wright made had stayed with me. It was about storytelling and how a possible meaning of freedom might reside not only in martial arts, in the ability to defend oneself, but in the ability to make oneself. Mas "taught me a lot of Eastern philosophy and gave me the means to become myself," Wright said. One day Mas told him about Tominaga Nakamoto. "He was a Japanese merchant philosopher," Wright told me. "I read translations of his stuff, material from the 1740s."

Weeks later, I was in the kitchen of the house Wright was renting in London, drinking tea with him, when I noticed a book on the countertop called *Visions of Virtue in Tokugawa Japan.* I'd done some mugging up by then and was keen to nail the name thing.

"So that's where you say you got the Nakamoto part?" I asked. "From the eighteenth-century iconoclast who criticized all the beliefs of his time?"

"Yes."

"What about Satoshi?"

"It means 'ash,'" he said. "The philosophy of Nakamoto is the neutral central path in trade. Our current system needs to be burned down and remade. That is what cryptocurrency does—it is the phoenix . . ."

"So 'satoshi' is the ash from which the phoenix . . ."

"Yes. And Ash is also the name of a silly Pokémon character. The guy with Pikachu." Wright smiled. "In Japan the name of Ash is Satoshi," he said.

"So, basically, you named the father of bitcoin after Pikachu's chum?"

"Yes," he said. "That'll annoy the buggery out of a few people." This was something he often said, as if annoying people was an art.

Wright's generation, now in their mid-to-late forties, are seeing a world that enlarges on their teenage kicks. For Wright, as for Jeff Bezos, the rules of how to shop and how to think and how to live are extrapolations of dreams they had sitting in a box room somewhere. "The person who experiences greatness must have a feeling for the myth he is in," Frank Herbert wrote in *Dune*, Wright's favorite novel as a teenager. "*Dune* was really about people," Wright told me. "It was about the idea that we don't want to leave things to machines and [should instead] develop as humans. But I see things a little differently from Mr. Herbert. I see that it's not one or the other—man or machines—it's a symbiosis and a way of becoming something different together." This kind of cyber-punk energy—as opposed to cypherpunk, an activist grouping that came later, with a specific interest in cryptography—delivered Wright's generation of would-be computer scientists into the brightness of the future.

After getting his first degree, Wright settled into IT roles in a number of companies. He became a well-known "go-to guy" among startups and security firms: he always solved the problem and they always came back for more. "When I've characterized Craig to colleagues and friends," Rob Jenkins, who worked with Wright in this period and now holds a senior position in Australia's Westpac Bank, told me, "I've always described him as the most qualified person I've ever known. I've worked with other smart people but Craig has such a strong desire to pursue knowledge. He has passion. And bitcoin was just another one of those bright things he was talking about."

"Sketch it out for me," I said to Wright. "Those years before bitcoin. What was happening that would later have an influence? I want to know about all the precursors, all the previous attempts to solve the problem."

"Back in 1997 there was Tim May's BlackNet . . ." May was a crypto-anarchist, who had been operating and agitating in the cypherpunk community since the mid-1980s. "Computer tech-nology is on the verge of providing the ability for individuals and groups to communicate and interact with each other in a totally anonymous manner," he wrote in the *Crypto-Anarchist Manifesto* in 1988. BlackNet operated like a precursor to WikiLeaks, soliciting secret information with payments made by untraceable, digital money.

"We all have a narcissistic hubris," Wright told me. He wanted to take May's BlackNet idea further. He was also enthusiastic, in those early days, about Hashcash and B-money. The idea behind Hashcash, a "proof of work" algorithm where each of a group of computers performs a small task that can be instantly verified (thus making life impossible for spammers, who depend on multiple e-mails going out with little to no work involved), was "totally necessary for the building of bitcoin." The Hashcash algorithm is like the system that asks you to type a short string of numbers and letters into a box when registering on some websites. Wright said that he spoke to Adam Back, who proposed Hashcash in 1997, "a few times in 2008, whilst setting up the first trials of the bitcoin protocol."

B-money was invented by a man called Wei Dai. At the time of its creation, Wei wrote a paper that assumed "the existence of an untraceable network, where senders and receivers are identified only by digital pseudonyms (public keys) and every message is signed by its sender and encrypted to its receiver." The public key, or address, is matched, writes John Lanchester in an essay on bitcoin, to "a private key which provides access to that address." A key is really just a string of numbers and letters: the public key demonstrates ownership of any given address; the private key can be used only by the owner of that address. Wei went on to suggest a system for the exchange and transfer of money. "Anyone can create money by broadcasting the solution to a previously unsolved computational problem," he wrote. The system had methods for rewarding work and keeping users honest. "I admired B-money,"

Wright told me, "and he definitely gave me some of the crypto-graphic code that ended up in the first version of bitcoin." Wright was always careful to give credit to those early developers. "Wei was very helpful," he went on, but "to people like that bit-coin seems a bit of a fudge. It works, but it's not mathematically elegant."

"Wei said that?"

"Wei was very polite. But others said it: Adam Back, Nick Szabo. They would probably like to find a more elegant solution to the problem. Perhaps they see the mining system in bitcoin as wasteful: there's wasted computation in my system—machines which are trying to solve problems and not winning. But that's like society."

"Are these early cryptocurrency people in a state of rivalry?"

"Yes, but it doesn't matter."

Kleiman

The flat in Marylebone where I interviewed Wright had wooden shutters and modern ornaments and pictures, mainly of crows. I set the flat up for work while Craig and Ramona were in the City signing over his intellectual property, and all his companies, to MacGregor. They arrived at the flat a couple of hours late. "When did you realize the whole Satoshi thing wasn't going to be a secret forever?" I asked.

"Very recently," Wright said. "I didn't really believe it would need to come out. What we believed is that we could leave it in doubt—we wouldn't have to sign using the Satoshi keys or any-thing else. We have hundreds of patents and papers in progress—research from the beginning—and in the next year we're going to start releasing them. We thought people could suspect and people could query and we could leave it like that."

"And how did that change?"

Ramona said a single word: "Rob."

The days in St. Christopher's Place were almost languorous. We would bring coffee back to the flat and spread out, and I'd try to build a picture of how he did what he said he did. We put up whiteboards and he bamboozled me with math. Sometimes he would write at the board for hours, then tear open books and point to theories and proofs. I talked to the scientists he worked with, many of whom were better explainers than he was. One of the things I noticed was that Wright hated claiming outright to be Satoshi and would spend hours giving credit to everyone who had ever contributed. It was odd: we were in the room because he was coming out as Satoshi, yet the claim embarrassed him and I have many hours of tape in which he deflects it. I felt this unwillingness supported his claim because it showed a proper regard for the communal nature of the work. He was contradictory enough sometimes to enjoy the limelight and actively court it, and this would cause trouble for him, but the idea of speaking directly as Satoshi seemed to fill him with dread. "I'm afraid that they're just going to look at my papers because I've got Satoshi after my name," he told me. "I've got my little Satoshi mask on, and people go, 'Aren't you wonderful (because you were Satoshi)?' I wanted the doubt. When I released future papers, I wanted people to go: 'Oh, fuck, he could be, and these papers are so good he might be.'"

Dave Kleiman was to become the most important person in Wright's professional life, the man he says helped him do Satoshi's work. They met online: they visited the same cryptography forums and had interacted since 2003. Both men were interested in cybersecurity, digital forensics, and the future of money, but Kleiman was a boy's boy, an army veteran who loved contact sports and fast living. Five foot ten and weighing 200 pounds, he lived in Riviera Beach, Florida, and from 1986 to 1990 he was an army helicopter technician. When I looked into Kleiman's life, I discovered he had also done computer forensics work for Homeland Security and the army. After active service he became a deputy in the Palm Beach County Sheriff's Office. A motorcycle crash in 1995, when he was twenty-eight, left him in a wheelchair. Kleiman was a drug user, and one source told me he was heavily into online gambling and various illicit activities; there is evidence he was associated with the Dark Web marketplace Silk Road. After the accident he devoted himself to computers, and set up a company called Computer Forensics LLC.

Until Napster (the brainchild of a teenager called Shawn Fanning) came along in 1999, enabling users to share music files across the Internet without a central server, the phrase "peer-to-peer sharing" was familiar only to the early Internet's true believers. Napster, with its user-friendly interface, brought file sharing to the masses. The old model of copyright and revenue generation became obsolete overnight: people stopped buying CDs; young people got music through the Internet for free. The music industry had to reinvent itself or die. Wright told me that his earliest conversations with Kleiman were about file sharing. In 2007 they wrote a study guide together on hacking. "I used to fire ideas off him," Wright said. "I'm pretty good at maths but I'm not very good at people." Kleiman, he said, could put up with his temper, which not everybody could. They began to speak of ways to use the Napster idea in other areas and solve some old problems in cryptography. Wright never, I have to say, made it fully clear how they had collaborated on building bitcoin. I kept returning to the subject, and my doubts would flare up when he failed to be explicit.

"Give me a sense of how the idea of Satoshi formed," I said.

"I guess," Wright replied, "the initial idea was having a pseudonymous head that wouldn't be cut off."

"More your idea than his?"

"Probably mine."

"And was there a point you realized you needed a figure-head?" I asked.

"We needed people to respond to us," he said. "But I didn't really want people to respond to me. There are a couple of reasons for that. I don't think I would really have sold the idea to anyone. If I'd come out originally as Satoshi without Dave, I don't think it would have gone anywhere. I've had too many conversations with people who get annoyed because it's me."

"The blockchain came about as an idea of a ledger," he later said. "But there were a number of problems that needed to be solved. It needed to be distributed, but how do you make sure people don't collude—it may seem awful but you don't put trust in people, you incentivize people to act. And you incentivize people to act by giving them the opportunity to earn something. It's as Adam Smith says: it's not through the goodness of the heart, it's not the baker caring about you, it's not the butcher caring about you, it's them caring about their own families. Together, as he put it, the invisible hand controls the way society works."

I asked him to explain the distributed ledger in layman's terms and he went into an algorithmic paroxysm of verbal ingenuity. Ignoring all that, a distributed ledger is a database that is shared among multiple users, with every contributor to the network having their own identical copy of the database. Any and all additions or alterations to the ledger are mirrored in every copy as soon as they're made. No central authority is in charge of it, but no entry on it can be disputed. Adam Smith's point about "incentive" is embedded in the way bitcoin works: people do not just buy coins or use them; they "mine" them. Miners use their computers to solve increasingly difficult mathematical problems, the reward for the solving of which can be paid in bitcoin. This keeps the currency honest and, ideally, stops it from being dominated by any single entity.

Again and again while we were speaking, he would jump up and cover the walls in formulae, along with arrows, arcs, and curves. His wife told me she sometimes goes into the shower room and finds him standing there, stark naked, writing on the steamed-up glass. "Was there a primary person doing the maths?" I asked.

"Me," he said. "Dave wasn't really a mathematician. What he did was make me simplify it."

"How did he know how to make you simplify it?"

"We got to a point in the writing of the Satoshi white paper where it was . . . People say that it was hard."

"He wanted you to bring the language down a little bit?"

"A lot. It's very simple. The elliptical curve stuff is not described in the paper at all, it's just there. The crypto stuff isn't described either." I asked him to show me the trail of ideas that led to their collaboration. "So all these things are there," he said, pointing to a 337-page thesis on his computer called "The Quantification of Information Systems Risk," which he had recently submitted in partial fulfilment of a philosophy doctorate at Charles Sturt University. "Application to audits, how you analyze failures, deriving the mathematics behind it, simplifying the mathematics, and there you go . . . The core of the bitcoin paper is a Poisson model based on binomial distribution. That's how it got solved."

In 2008 it was a "hodgepodge," he said. I asked him if he felt the development of bitcoin was, at some level, a response to the financial crisis. "It was already in process. I saw [the crisis] coming, though. It was a kind of perfect storm. During that year, I spoke to Wei Dai. So between him and Hal Finney there were a lot of really good ideas about making money work . . . [Finney] was the one who actually took what I said seriously. He received the first bitcoin."

Wright started turning up to our interviews in a three-piece suit. His suits were unfashionable and his ties even more so— 1970s-style yellow, sometimes paisley—and he would ramble on a range of subjects. On his own subject, he could be brilliant, but he was wayward: he would sidetrack, miss the point, and never come back to it. He was nothing like people imagine the mythical Satoshi to be—in fact, he was Satoshi's comic opposite. He told stories against himself that weren't really against himself. He was obsessed with his opponents' views but had no skill at providing a straight answer to their questions. "I'm an arsehole," he said many times, as if saying so were a major concession. But he wasn't really, he was actually pretty nice. He was arrogant about math and computing, which wasn't so surprising. He also had a habit of dissembling, of now and then lying about small things in a way that cast shade on larger things. At one point, I asked him to send me an e-mail from the original Satoshi account.

"Can you do that?" I asked.

"Yes," he said. "But I'd need Rob's permission." When I asked MacGregor he said that was absurd. Wright simply didn't want to—or couldn't—give too much away, and that was unfortunate in someone who'd agreed to sit down every day with a writer. He seemed to have full knowledge of that e-mail account, in a way that made it unquestionably his. But somehow, it offended his sense of personal power to prove it. At first, I thought he was a man in existential crisis, like the hero of Bellow's *Dangling Man*, brilliant but antisocial, waiting to be drafted. But as the months passed I began to think of him more as a Russian "superfluous" man of the 1850s, a romantic hero out of Turgenev, constantly held back from self-realization by some blinding secret, showing himself not by action but in speech. Wright talked all day and he scribbled on the board and he called me his friend. He cried and he shouted and he unloaded his childhood and spoke about his father. He claimed to be Satoshi and he spoke Satoshi's thoughts and described what he did and gave an account of what people misunderstood about his invention and where bitcoin needed to go now. I moved to an office in Piccadilly—it was like something out of John le Carré, all those rooftops and fluttering Union Jacks—and we continued to do interviews. He talked without cease, without direction, and continued to find it difficult to land near the spot where my question was marked on the ground. When I asked to see the e-mails between him and Kleiman, he shrugged. He said he wasn't getting on well with his first wife when he wrote them, and I assumed that meant they were full of talk about her. "Just edit them down for me," I said.

"I don't know if I can find them," he said. But I wouldn't let it go and eventually he sent me a selection and they certainly seem to be authentic. A few of the e-mails were obviously the same as those quoted in the *Wired* and *Gizmodo* stories before Christmas. Wright always said these stories had been provoked by a "leak," the work of a disgruntled employee of his who had stolen a hard drive. In any case, the e-mails he sent me show a pair of men with shadowy habits—socially undernourished men, I'd say, with a high degree of intellectual ability—operating in a world where the line between inventing and scamming is not always clear. The first e-mail Wright sent me was from November 27, 2007, when he was working for the Sydney accountancy firm BDO Kendalls and the two men were working on a paper, "Cookies in Internet Banking." "Next year Dave, we come out with something big. I will tell you, but not now," he wrote to Kleiman on December 22, 2007. Kleiman's reply told him what he was reading—"Sagan, Feynman, Einstein"—and added: "I hope we make an event together this year so we can 'break some bread' and have a casual conversation, instead of the brain dump middle of the night email exchanges we normally have." On January 1, 2008, Wright closed an e-mail: "Nothing now, but I want your help on something big soon."

The subject of bitcoin came up—quite starkly—in an e-mail from Wright dated March 12, 2008: "I need your help editing a paper I am going to release later this year. I have been working on a new form of electronic money. Bit cash, bitcoin . . . you are always there for me Dave. I want you to be part of it all. I cannot release it as me. GMX, vistomail and Tor. I need your help and I need a version of me to make this work that is better than me." Wright told me that he did the coding and that Kleiman helped him to write the white paper and make the language "serene." With a protocol as clever as the one underlying bitcoin, you would imagine the work was complex and endlessly discussed. But Wright says they mainly talked about it by direct message and by phone. Wright was being let go from his job at BDO (the crash was taking effect) and was in the process of retiring with his then wife, Lynn, and many computers, to a farm in Port Macquarie. It was there, Wright says, that he did the majority of the work on bitcoin and where he spoke to Kleiman most regularly. The Satoshi white paper, "Bitcoin: A Peer-to-Peer Electronic Cash System," was published on a cryptography mailing list on October 31, 2008.

On December 27, 2008, Wright wrote to Kleiman: "My wife will not be happy, but I am not going back to work. I need time to get my idea going . . . The presentation was good and the paper is out. I am already getting shit from people and attacks on what we did. The bloody bastards are wrong and I friken showed it, they should stick to the science and piss off with their politicized crap. I need your help. You edited my paper and now I need to have you aid me build this idea." Wright told me that it took several attempts to get the protocol up and running. He began to test it early in January 2009. "That was where the real money started rolling in," he told me. The originating block in the blockchain—the file that provably records every transaction ever made—is called the Genesis block. "There were actually a few versions of the Genesis block," Wright told me. "It fucked up a few times and we reviewed it a few times. The Genesis block is the one that didn't crash." There from the beginning was Hal Finney, who would receive the first bitcoin transaction, on block 9. This was a key moment for the new cryptocurrency: block 9 forever shows that Satoshi sent Finney ten bitcoins on January 12, 2009—it is the first outgoing transaction we know to have come from Satoshi. Satoshi also sent four other transactions on the same day. I asked Wright who the recipients were—who the four addresses belonged to. "Hal, Dave, myself," he replied. "And another I cannot name as I have no right to do so." Wright told me that around this time he was in correspondence with Wei Dai, with Gavin Andresen, who would go on to lead the development of bitcoin, and with Mike Hearn, a Google engineer who had ideas about the direction bitcoin should take. Yet when I asked for copies of the e-mails between Satoshi and these men he said they had been wiped when he was running from the ATO. It seemed odd, and still does, that some e-mails were lost while others were not. I think he believed it would be more interesting to play hide-and-seek than to be a man with a knowable past.

Wright's e-mails to Kleiman suggest that by this point he was starting to mine the million or so bitcoins that are said to be owned by Satoshi Nakamoto. "I have a few potential clients in gaming and banking," he wrote to Kleiman. "I figure I can work ten to 15 hours a week and pretend to have a consultancy and use this to build and buy the machines I need. If I automate the code and monitoring, I can double the productivity and still offer more than others are doing . . . The racks are in place in Bagnoo and Lisarow. I figure we can have 100 cores a month setup and get to around 500."

Kleiman replied the same day to affirm their vows. "Craig, you always know I am there for you. You changed the paradigm that was held for over a decade and destroyed the work of a couple academics. Do you really think they will just take this happily? I know you will not, but try not to take the comments to heart. Let the paper speak for itself. Next time you need to get me a copy of the conference proceedings as well. You know it is not easy for me to travel." A picture emerges of an ailing Kleiman sitting at his computer day and night in his small ranch-style house in Riviera Beach, Florida. After writing this last e-mail, he spent a frighteningly long period in hospital. The two men agreed to meet up at a conference in Florida on March 11, 2009, and Kleiman wrote expressing his excitement at the prospect of a few beers with Wright. Craig and Lynn stayed at Disney's Coronado Springs Resort Hotel, and Kleiman drove there in his customized van, rolling into the bar with a big smile: Kleiman was the brother and drinking buddy and like-minded computer nerd Wright had never had. Not even Lynn had a clue what they were talking about.

During my visit to Australia I met Lynn in Chatswood, on Sydney's north shore, a busy commercial district that heaves with eager shoppers on a Saturday morning. She had met Wright on the Internet while she was working as the nursing manager of the ICU in a military hospital in Ottawa. She told me Wright asked her to marry him about six weeks after they met online. When she eventually went to Sydney to visit him, he brought a ring to the airport. "He was twenty-six and I was forty-four," she said. Neither of them had been married before.

"He was very mature for twenty-six," Lynn told me. "He always has to be the best. And the hard part about that is he left bodies by the wayside. He stepped on people." She began working for him—"he was the geek and I was the gofer"—and he got a lot of work in information security, working for the Australian Securities Exchange and for Centrebet, which was where he first got to know Stefan Matthews. Wright told me he was afraid some of the things he did for those online betting companies would come back to bite him, if and when he was outed as Satoshi. Other sources told me that he and Kleiman had had some involvement with illegal gambling. "I knew Dave Kleiman and he were working together," Lynn told me, "and I remember them saying that digital money was the way of the future. I've never said this to anybody, but I knew he was working on it and I didn't ask, because I knew he would bite my head off if I didn't understand it. He's got a very sociopathic personality."

Lynn said her husband had admired Kleiman. And she admired him, too: "He loved life," she said, "and he had a brilliant mind, like Craig, but he had a gentler soul." She remembered the Orlando conference. "We stayed in a hotel that looked like a giant cartoon," she told me. "We met in one of the bars. He was a young guy, in his thirties or early forties, brown hair and mustache, average-looking. And boy, he loved to have a good time. It might have been his birthday. I went into the Disney store and bought some hats—Craig had Pluto, and Dave had one in the shape of a giant birthday cake." Wright stepped out of himself for Kleiman: "I'd never seen him like that with anybody. It was like, 'I wanna grow up to be just like him.' Dave softened Craig. A lot of what they wrote together was in his voice. I'd never seen Craig react like that to anybody. When he felt unsure of himself he went and talked to Dave. I think he wanted to be like Dave, but he knew he couldn't be."

"In terms of having that kind of temperament?"

"Yeah. Dave was good for him. It made him realize that life doesn't go your way all of the time."

I asked her if she thought Craig was a flawed person. "Yes," she said. "He's starting to realize it. He knows he's done well in his work but he hasn't done well as a human being." She stared into her cup. "When we were at the farm," she said, "I was interested in finding four-leaf clovers. I would never find any, but Craig would just step out of the house and find three."

In mid-2011 Satoshi suddenly disappeared from view. Apart from one or two e-mails denouncing fake Satoshis, he wasn't heard from again. Control of the network alert key is said to have been passed at this time to Andresen—possession of this key makes its holder the closest thing bitcoin has to a chief. Wright sent Kleiman an e-mail on September 10, 2011: "It is recorded. I cannot do the Satoshi bit any more. They no longer listen. I am better as a myth. Back to my lectures and rants that everyone ignores as me. I hate this Dave, my pseudonym is more popular than I can ever hope to be."

For some reason—possibly fear of the ATO—Wright set up a trust fund called the Tulip Trust in June 2011, and asked Kleiman to sign an agreement stating that he, Kleiman, would hold 1,100,111 bitcoins (then valued at £100,000, currently worth around $800 million). For clarity: there is no evidence that Kleiman ever took custody of that amount. However, there was a separate agreement that Kleiman would receive 350,000 bitcoins and this transaction was made. "All bitcoin will be returned to Dr Wright on 1 January 2020," it says in the trust document.

> No record of this arrangement will be made public at any time . . . Dr Wright MAY request a loan of bitcoin for the following reasons (and no others): Furthering research into peer to peer systems . . . commercial activities that enhance the value and position of bitcoin. In all events, all transactions in loaned funds will be concluded outside of Australia and the USA until and unless a clear and acceptable path to the recognition of bitcoin as currency has occurred . . . I lastly acknowledge that I will not divulge the identity of the Key with ID C941FE6D nor of the origins of the satoshin@gmx.com e-mail.

Kleiman signed it. "I think you are mad and this is risky," he wrote in an e-mail to Wright on June 24, 2011, perhaps spying a possible illegality. "But I believe in what we are trying to do." Wright meanwhile seemed to get more and more frustrated. He both wanted fame and repudiated it, craving the recognition he felt was his due while claiming his only wish was to get back to his desk. "I have people who love my secret identity and hate me," he wrote to Kleiman on October 23 that year. "I have hundreds of papers. Satoshi has one. Nothing, just one bloody paper and I cannot associate myself with ME! I am tired of all these dicks Dave. Tired of academic attacks. Tired of tax fuckwits. Tired of having to do shenanigans like moving stuff overseas IN CASE it works."

I came to feel that there were secrets between Wright and Kleiman that might never be revealed. Wright usually clammed up when asked about Kleiman and money. One day, in a fit of high spirits, he showed me a piece of software he said that U.S. Homeland Security had ripped off from him and Kleiman. He smiled when I asked if they'd done government security work. The first thing most people ask about when you mention Satoshi is his alleged bitcoin hoard: he invented the thing, and created the Genesis block, and mined bitcoins from the start, so where was Wright's money and where was Kleiman's? The e-mails, when I got them, seemed to clear this up slightly, but during many dozens of hours of conversation with Wright, he never properly told me how many bitcoins he mined. (Mining, by the way, creates no real-world benefit. It is simply the process by which computers are set, by the miners, to burn up energy solving math problems, in order to gain a "reward" with a designated "value": one bitcoin.) I was aware—and he knew I was aware, because I told him several times—that he wasn't giving me a full account of everything that had occurred between him and Kleiman. He said it was complicated.

Somewhat more helpful are minutes taken during a meeting between the ATO and representatives from Wright's Australian companies in Sydney on February 26, 2014. According to the minutes, Wright's representative John Cheshire went into detail about the financial collaboration between Wright and Kleiman. This was a story that Wright, for some reason, didn't want to tell me. Cheshire said that Wright and Kleiman had set up a company called W&K Info Defense LLC (W&K), "an entity created for the purpose of mining bitcoins." Some of these bitcoins were put into a Seychelles trust and some into one in Singapore. Wright, according to Cheshire, "had gotten approximately 1.1 million bitcoins. There was a point in time when he had around 10 per cent of all the bitcoins out there. Mr Kleiman would have had a similar amount."

I asked Wright about this and he told me it was true that his and Kleiman's mining activity had led to a complicated trust. The trust question was persistently vague: not only how many trusts but the names of the trustees and the dates of their formation. The only consistent thing is the number of bitcoins Wright is said to have had at one time, 1.1 million. He said that these holdings could not now be moved without the agreement of the (several) trustees. He also said that Kleiman had been given 350,000 bitcoins but had not moved them. He kept them on a personal hard drive.

Wright also set up a shell company in the UK. "I know what you want and I know how impatient you can be," Kleiman wrote on December 10, 2012, "but really, we need to do this right. If you fail you can start again. That is the real beauty of what you have." It's possible Kleiman was referring to their ability to mine bitcoins and then squirrel them away. But he was evidently worried about Wright's ability to cope with all the flak, and about Wright's kamikaze attitude to the tax authorities. "I love you like a brother Craig," he added, "but you are a really difficult person to be close to. You need people. Stop pushing them away. You have over one million bitcoin now in the trust. Start doing something for yourself and this family you have."

Around this time, an eighteen-year-old IT enthusiast called Uyen Nguyen began working with them. Very quickly, Kleiman made her a co-director of their company, and she later became a powerful figure in the trust. It's unclear how such a young and inexperienced person came to have so much influence. Wright told me she was "volatile, capricious, and beyond control." He added that Kleiman liked young women and that she was loyal and trusted—but that "she wants to help and this always leads to trouble." While I was preparing this story, Wright began to seem worried about Nguyen. I always felt he was in the middle of a very complicated lie when he talked about her. "My way of lying," he told me one day, "is to let you believe something. If you stop questioning and then you go off, and I don't correct you—that's my lie."

Toward the end of 2012, Dave began to fail. "Paraplegics get sick a lot," Lynn Wright had told me, speaking as a nurse. "The bedsores get bad and they can't fight infections. Dave was in and out of hospital a lot and I don't know what his life was really like." Wright told me that Kleiman had girlfriends, but admitted he didn't really know much about his life. Like Wright and his first wife, they had met in a chatroom. They met in the flesh no more than half a dozen times. Kleiman seems to have lived in front of his computer day and night, and the sicker he got, the more isolated he seemed to be. Just after 6:00 p.m. on April 27, 2013, he was found dead by a friend who'd been trying to contact him for several days. He was sitting in his wheelchair and leaning to the left with his head resting on his hand. Lying next to him on the bed were a .45-caliber semiautomatic handgun, a bottle of whiskey, and a loaded magazine of bullets. In the mattress a few feet from where he sat, a bullet hole was found, but Kleiman had died from coronary heart disease. There were prescription medicines in his bloodstream and a modest amount of cocaine.

"We never really thought that we 'made Satoshi,'" Wright told me once. "It was good. It was done. It was cool. But I don't think we realized how big it would be."

"There was no conversation between you about how it was going over? That Satoshi was becoming a guru?"

"We thought it was funny."

Wright paused, shook his head, and broke down. "I loved Dave," he said. "I would have seen him more. I would have talked to him more. I would've made sure he had some fucking money to go to a decent hospital. I don't think he had the right to choose not to tell me."

"What was happening to him?"

"Neither of us had any money, physical money. We had money in Liberty, an exchange in Costa Rica, but the Americans closed it down as a money-laundering operation. Dave had a number of bitcoins on the hard drive he carried with him. Probably about three hundred and fifty thousand."

"Hoping it would . . ."

"As I said, it wasn't worth that much then. Dave died a week before the value went up by twenty-five times." Wright kept wiping his eyes and shaking his head. He emphasized something he said the commentators never understood: for a long time, bitcoin wasn't worth anything, and they constantly needed money to keep the whole operation going. They feared that dumping their bitcoin hoard would have flooded the market and devalued the currency. One of the things Wright and Kleiman had in common was that they had a problem turning their ideas into cash and were always being chased by creditors. Kleiman died feeling like a failure. No one in his family has the passwords to release the bitcoins on his computer. After he died, his family didn't open probate on his estate because they believed it had no value. Kleiman's supposed personal bitcoin holdings are worth $260 million at today's prices.

The London Office

No one in London seemed too bothered by the earlier rubbishing of Craig Wright. The computer technology world had dismissed him after the *Wired* "outing" of him in December 2015, but Wright and the company just marched on, with the help of an expensive PR company, preparing for the big reveal that would prove the naysayers wrong. The company behind the deal, nCrypt, was investing more and more in Wright at this point, and they were desperate for the story that I kept saying wasn't close to being ready. It required absolute proof, and not even they, by their own admission, had quite seen that yet. But they continued to build him up. In January 2016, on a rainy London afternoon, Wright took me to see the large office that was being set up for him as part of the deal with nCrypt. It hadn't taken long for the world to forget that they'd once thought Wright was Satoshi. One or two of the media organizations that had "outed" him in December had taken down the original articles from their websites, stung by the cries of fraud. After only a few days' interest in the notion, most people had made up their minds that Wright had nothing to do with Satoshi. Wright—under strict advisement—had said nothing in response to the media reports accusing him of perpetrating a hoax, but when we were alone, which was most of the time, he would launch into point-by-point rebuttals of what his critics had been saying. In the end he would shrug, as if the most obscure things were actually obvious.

The press coverage of Wright and Wright himself had something in common: they succeeded in making him seem less plausible than he actually was, and, to me, that is a general truth about computer geeks. They are content to know what they know and not to explain it. They will answer a straightforward slur with an algorithm, or fail to claim credit for something big then spend all night trying to claim credit for something small. Many of the accusations of lying that were thrown at Wright that December were thrown by other coders. And that's what they're like—see Reddit, or any of the bitcoin forums. Much of what these people do they do in the dark, beyond scrutiny, and, just as it's against their nature to incriminate themselves, it is equally unnatural for them, even under pressure, to de-incriminate themselves. They just shrug.

Coders call one another liars, when all they really mean is that they disagree about how software should work. During the time I was working with Wright in secret, I would text my colleague John Lanchester, who I knew I could trust to keep the secret but also to understand what was at stake in the story. "Imagine a situation," I wrote to John, "where novelists were strangely invested in denying the plausibility of each other's books. There's no 'proof' as such that one is right and the other is wrong, but they could argue fiercely and accuse each other of all sorts of things while not really settling the problem."

"Edmund Wilson says somewhere that the reason poets dislike each other's books is because they seem wrong, false—a kind of lie," John replied. "If you were telling the truth you would be writing the same poems as me."

So the world that Wright knew best thought he was a liar. And the day we visited his new offices he seemed resigned to the fact. Much later, he told me that these months were the high point of his career in computer science: he was working in secret on material that seemed to be coming together beautifully and profitably. It irked him that people called him a fraud and it irked him, just as much, that his deal with nCrypt would require him to prove that he was Satoshi. He hated being accused of being a fraud *and* he hated having to prove that he wasn't a fraud. Having it both ways is a life, a life that requires a certain courage as well as shamelessness, and Wright was living his double life to the hilt.

Wright introduced me to Allan Pedersen, who'd been his project manager in Sydney. We were in the Workshop—a floor above MacGregor's office near Oxford Circus—standing at a glass workbench beside a whiteboard covered in writing. The opposite wall was stenciled with a quote from Henry Ford: "Whether you think you can or think you can't, you are right." Pedersen told me he had been brought over to direct a group preparing an initial batch of thirty-two patent applications, to be completed by April 2016. (This was in January of that year.) Beyond that there were "upwards of four hundred patents," ideas to do with using the blockchain to set up contracts that would come into action on specified dates years ahead, or using the blockchain to allow cars to tell their owners when they needed gasoline and to debit the cost when they refueled. At this point, and for several minutes afterward, Wright spoke of himself in the third person. "Craig has been given a big kick up the bum," he said, "because Craig, instead of doing tons of research and sticking it on a shelf, has to complete it and turn it into something."

"How do you organize him?" I asked Pedersen.

"I'm the organized type," he said. "When Craig comes into the office he's always in the middle of a sentence. And I'm trying to work out what this sentence is and manage things around what he's saying. I'm sort of grounding his latest thoughts, placing them in what we're trying to do. I'm the glue between Craig and the developers."

It had become obvious, mainly from things Wright himself had said, that he often found it difficult to get along with people who worked for him. He got rattled when they said things couldn't be done, or were too conventional in their thinking, or too stupid, as he saw it. Ramona told me that 40 percent of his staff in Sydney had been in a state of rebellion. "I'm an arsehole," Craig said to me once again, "and I know that." Pedersen had the job of keeping things cool with the developers, whose job it was to turn Wright's ideas into a form in which they could be patented and eventually licensed. "I'm making sure the ideas get executed," he said. "Craig's not that interested in that part. He's always moving on."

"Craig's great at research," Wright said of himself, "but his development and commercialization sucks. I build it, and then it works, and then I walk off."

"You're losing interest?"

"I've lost interest. I've proved it, and off I go."

"It's getting easier," Pedersen said, with a smile. "It was quite complex in the beginning." Wright had strong views about how the technology should develop, and how it could "scale" to meet greater demand. "It can go to any size," Wright said that day. "I've tested up to 340-gigabyte blocks, which is hundreds of thousands of times greater than it is now. It's every stock exchange, it's every registry rolled into one . . . Ultimately bitcoin is a 1980s program, because that's what I was trained in . . . The idea is good, the code is robust, it runs and does the job, but it's slow and cumbersome. There were some things early on that needed to be fixed and were, but it wasn't as perfect as everyone thinks. At the end of the day, it needs to be turned into professional code. It needs to move away from the home user network and into a server network environment. And then it can do much more and be faster." There are those who feel it should remain small, and that making it bigger is a betrayal of its first principles.

"This is the future of the blockchain," Pedersen said.

"People are saying, 'It's not really something we can run yet,'" Wright said, "but it's time that we grew up and that bitcoin becomes professional."

Pedersen shook his head. "We're not working in a world where we know exactly what we're doing," he said. "It's coming from Craig. And then I start establishing the ground rules and we begin rolling it out. I'm putting people on a certain track and I keep going back to Craig, saying, 'We need to sort this or that out,' and I'm constantly keeping them and him in the loop. The good thing about Craig is that he wants me to task him, so it's a very strange relationship we've got. I'm reporting to him but I'm tasking him at the same time and it seems to work beautifully." He was tired, and so was the whole team, but they felt confident the patent applications would be filed on time.

When Craig left the room to take a phone call, Pedersen took pains to close the door properly. "He's a really nice person," he said, "but he's a fucking nightmare. Every single morning he comes in and I think, 'What is he talking about?'" Pedersen told me how he handled him, how he made him focus, and how he worked hard to keep him on track. "When I've got new people here," he said, and there were many new people, "I have to train them how to talk to Craig. That's what I have to do. Sometimes, he can't explain things and this is where the anger comes from. It's the interesting part. You can't be in the same room with him. He's constantly telling you something. He's like Steve Jobs, you know—only worse."

As we made our way to the new office—it was a construction site that day, but would be up and running four weeks later— Wright presented himself as a man who was ready for anything. In a pin-striped suit and ruby tie, he looked like a hellbent 1980s bond dealer, except the cypherpunk glint in the eye suggested he was getting away with something. He wasn't the king of all he surveyed, he was the joker, and, crossing Oxford Street, he joked that he might be Moses. The traffic parted and he made his way to the promised land, a brand-new suite of offices down a side street.

Pedersen had come along. "This is how it works in this company," he said. "You're sitting in Vancouver in October"—Vancouver is where nTrust, the parent company, is based—"and suddenly Rob MacGregor says: 'We need these thirty-odd patents by April and when can you go to London?'" The hurry for the patents was to help with the giant sale to Google or whomever. The men behind the deal were very keen to beat other blockchain developers to the punch, especially the R3 consortium of banks and financial institutions, which late in 2015 started spending a fortune trying to deploy the technology. We were accompanied by a young Irishwoman who had been put in charge of designing the new office. MacGregor's firm had invested millions in Wright. The new company, nCrypt, had pretty much been built around him, and its offices showed it. He was to have the enormous corner office with a view all the way along Oxford Street. MacGregor clearly believed in Wright, however obnoxious he could be, but I never understood why he wasn't interrogating his uncertainties before spending his money. He was a lawyer, but he put trust in front of diligence, which is unusual in someone so intelligent. MacGregor never, incidentally, used the words "off the record" with me—only once, later on, did he imply it, when he said something and then said he'd deny saying it if I quoted him—and he was a generous source of information. At no point, however, did he tell me where the money for this project was coming from.

The designer was waving a color swatch. "We've gone for a kind of Scandi look," she said.

"This place will work," Wright said, striding through the open space, "mainly when it comes to protecting me from myself." Amid the hammering and drilling, Wright stood in an office about twenty feet by twenty feet, with floor-to-ceiling windows and a view down into the heart of Soho.

"You remember J. R. Ewing in *Dallas*?" I asked.

Wright laughed. What he most enjoyed, he said, was that all this was going on in secret while the world outside had written him off as a mug and a fantasist. "If Satoshi has to come out, he'll come out in style." He turned back to the designer to tell her how the frosted glass should work in the meeting room. "We do a lot of work on whiteboards," he said. He pursed his lips, then smiled. "Will the interactive whiteboards be set up so that I can contact the guys in Sydney?"

We spent an hour at the new office. "And they say *nothing is going on*," Wright said as we stepped back into the elevator. "It's all a *figment of our imagination*. I'm not Satoshi, and none of this is real." Out on the street again, he told me he had all the money he would ever need. "And I'll have the monkeys off my back forever and just get on with the one thing I'm good at, not business, not managing people, but doing research and honoring this thing we made." Wright was enjoying himself, but nCrypt was already, as MacGregor told me repeatedly, negotiating the sale of the whole package to the highest bidder: "Buy in, sell out, make some zeroes," as he had said, and he'd always been honest about that goal. Wright wasn't facing up to this. The next time I visited his corner office it was finished and decked out with claret-red leather armchairs and sofas flown in from Sydney. It looked, as I'd joked earlier, like the office of a Texan oil magnate. A host of management certificates were framed on the wall next to a signed photograph of Muhammad Ali.

I told Pedersen I thought Wright was struggling with the fine print of the deal—coming out. "He's sold his soul," Pedersen said. "That's how simple this is. And the combination of Craig and Ramona is dangerous here. They can't just sign all these [legal] papers and think it's going to be all right, that they'll sort something out. It doesn't work that way. They now have to go to the end and live with it. But they're doing it on first class. When this Satoshi thing comes out I can see a lot of bad things happening, and they are not geared up for this, any of them."

"I'm concerned for him," I said.

"There's not really a happy ending here," Pedersen said.

"Was it the same in Australia?"

"It was the exact same," he said, "except in Australia you could say he was in control. He's learned absolutely nothing. He's now in this box, he can't move, he can't do anything, and this box is getting smaller and smaller."

"Do you think he wants to be outed as Satoshi?"

"Yes, I do. It's in in his personality. He wants to be recognized. He says too much. After two weeks of working with him, I knew."

"He and Ramona tell me they had a pact never to come out."

"My feeling is that she doesn't want him to come out, but he does. He's been pushing for this to happen."

I spoke to one of the scientists, a shy, unexcitable man in his late fifties, who had been working on this technology for several years. He and Pedersen are old-school IT people, quiet-spoken and completely uninterested in the limelight. Both of them thought Wright was working at a different level from everybody else. The scientist, who spoke to me from the beginning on the condition that he wouldn't be named, worried about Wright's attention to detail and about his conspiratorial nature, but he had no doubts about Wright's command of the big picture. The scientist was helping to oversee all the white papers and patent applications and managing a large team of IT specialists and mathematicians. I asked him if he was worried about the R3 consortium's work on blockchain technology. "They are going to fail," he said. "They don't have Satoshi. There is a panic out there, a misunderstanding about how the blockchain and bitcoin works. They hire people who know about bitcoin and are attempting to buy into it rather than being left behind. I've read some patent applications that are pending, applied for by the Bank of America. What I saw was ultimately unimpressive in comparison to what Craig is trying to do with the blockchain."

The scientist described how the staff try to get the ideas out of

Wright's head: "You can't say: 'Explain this to me.' If you ask a question like that, he'll just go off on giant tangents. First, he'll have difficulty explaining what's in his head. Often he's just coming up with ideas on the spot that he'll throw into conversation. You want to try to get yes-and-no answers from him. We film him at the whiteboard and someone will type out the text."

He described moments when everyone in the research team thought what Wright was saying was impossible. It couldn't be done, the software wasn't up to it, the blockchain couldn't scale to the task, and then suddenly everyone would understand what he was saying and appreciate its originality. "I need to be able to go over what he's said," the scientist told me, "to find the pearls of wisdom and find out what the hell he means. If I don't get it then I might have to make some guesses. I had to train my team to work in that mode. They have to be good researchers. They have to *understand* the technology as well as be able to work with it."

Often, the scientist said, the staff were amazed by an unexpected turn in Wright's thinking. But he admitted to being amazed, too, by certain gaps in Wright's technical knowledge. It was bizarre. Wright had what the scientist and the team regarded as vast experience and command of the blockchain, which he spoke of as his invention and appeared to know inside out, but then he would file a piece of math that didn't work. Or he would show a lack of detailed knowledge of something the team took for granted. Nobody I spoke to could explain this discrepancy. "One of the problems with him is that he's a terrible communicator," the scientist said. "He's invented this beautiful thing—the Internet of value. But sometimes he'll just talk in equations but can't or is unwilling to explain their content and application." His mistakes could also, he implied, be a result of laziness and lack of attention to detail.

I knew this for myself, but I was, to some extent, vexed that the technologists had the same experience. At the same time, I was impressed that people like the scientist and Pedersen could live with such a high degree of ambivalence about their boss. When I asked Pedersen if he thought the work was truly revolutionary, a non-native weariness came into his blue eyes. "I think so," he said. "But I don't think he'll get the Nobel Prize because he's too political. He's coming out as a street fighter and could end up in prison or whatever."

The main players in this story were keen to help me, to talk about what they knew and to show me the documents, but, in every case, there were topics they would avoid, and that were never cleared up. One of the most helpful individuals was Stefan Matthews. He pointed me in the direction of people from Wright's personal life, and sent me a typed history of his association with the man who would be Satoshi. Matthews noted that when Wright signed the deal with MacGregor, he didn't have a feasible business plan for any of his companies. The Wrights' financial situation was dire. They couldn't pay their staff and a number had already left. Pedersen and some others had stayed on without pay; Wright owed his lawyers $1 million Australian. Superannuation remittances were overdue and loan repayments unpaid; the companies needed the equivalent of £200,000 just to make it to next week. Craig and Ramona had sold their cars. One of the companies was already in receivership and, with the ATO closing in, "all related entities were on the brink of collapse." Before signing the deal, MacGregor, sources say, tried to assess the value of Wright's research, commissioning a "high-level overview" of the companies. MacGregor instructed Matthews to be in Sydney on June 24, 2015, when a final appraisal of the businesses was undertaken and a draft arrangement negotiated for nTrust "to acquire the intellectual property and the companies themselves."

One night I went to have dinner with Matthews on my own. We met in the restaurant at the back of Fortnum & Mason, on Jermyn Street, and he seemed incongruous among the red banquettes—a large, bald Australian with a rough laugh and wearing a plaid shirt, keen to tell me everything he thought useful. Matthews seemed a much more affable character than MacGregor, both upfront and very loyal, without perhaps seeing how the two might cancel each other out. One of the tasks of the eager businessman is to make himself more sure of his own position, and Matthews spent a lot of time, as did MacGregor, selling the idea of Wright as Satoshi rather than investigating it. They drafted me into telling the world who Wright was, but they didn't really know for sure themselves, and at one point their seeming haste threatened to drive a wedge between us. It seemed odd that they would ask a writer to celebrate a truth without first providing overwhelming evidence that the truth was true. I took it in my stride, most of the time, and enjoyed the doubts, while hoping for clarity.

Matthews drank a little wine but not much. He was talking about the night in Sydney when they signed the deal. "We pulled up outside Rob's hotel. He said: 'Do you realize what you have just done? You have just done the deal of a career. This is a billion-dollar deal. Fucking more. Billion dollars plus.'"

"Why is Rob so convinced?"

"Don't know, don't know." (MacGregor later told me he was convinced because Wright had shown Matthews the draft Satoshi white paper. "I always had that," MacGregor said.) "If it turns out that he's a fraud, I don't know how he's managed to do it, because you couldn't make this up."

Matthews told me about a meeting at the Bondi Iceberg Club in Sydney that Wright had with Ross Ulbricht, the founder of Silk Road, now serving two life sentences. Silk Road used bitcoin to trade all kinds of contraband items because the transactions could be made anonymously. Wright later confirmed that this meeting took place, but said only that Ulbricht was full of himself and they didn't discuss bitcoin. Matthews seemed to think this was unlikely. He wondered whether Kleiman had had more to do with Ulbricht; other sources suggested the same.

"Wright signed a deal to come out as Satoshi," I said to Matthews. "Does he realize everything that involves?"

"You're gonna have criminal groups that paid him lots of money and there are people who know about that," Matthews alleged. "If they quack? You've got Ross Ulbricht, who's in prison and apparently going to appeal trial this year or next. What happens when Ross sees Satoshi's name splashed everywhere and Craig's name everywhere? Is he going to say 'I had lunch with that guy. We made a deal'? I'm not worried about what Craig has done, I worry about people who have associated with him." It was very strange to do an interview with someone who would come out with this stuff, given that he was also trying to market the guy. In fairness to Wright, Matthews might just have been running his mouth off, and I've left out the worst of what he said, now and later.

We talked about some of the difficulties that had arisen between Wright and MacGregor. "Craig and Ramona are in a state about the keys leaving the room," I said. "He feels it is an act of self-annihilation to let them go. Rob has a Hollywood ending in mind and it's looking incredibly unlikely. You can't go into a marketplace claiming full legitimacy when the proof hasn't been produced." I told Matthews that there were e-mails still missing between Wright and Kleiman, e-mails that the public would want to see before accepting him as Satoshi, because the correspondence would presumably go into the kind of detail about the invention that only the inventors could know. Wright had told me he would produce the missing e-mails by the following Wednesday, but he never did.

"I know what's in there," Matthews told me. "It will be chatter to do with illegal stuff that he and Dave were doing in Costa Rica—particularly around Costa Rican casinos where they got $23 million of income. And you don't get paid that amount just for doing a security review . . . He mined all those bitcoins himself using equipment that he bought with money that he got from Costa Rica." Again: Why was Matthews saying this? It was obvious to me that Wright was going to have a problem telling the full story, whatever it was. I wasn't even sure he'd told the full story to his wife, but perhaps he had, because she referred, several times, to the fact that there were things that she just couldn't tell me. "They'll come after us," she said, in a state of high emotion. "They'll destroy us." Matthews said he didn't know what that was about. He did tell me something he said he had told MacGregor when MacGregor asked him what he was getting out of the deal. "Absolutely nothing," Matthews said. "I get what I get paid by Calvin. Calvin is the only allegiance I have, then and now."

Calvin Ayre is one of the topics the team routinely went dark on. When I first met Wright, he called him "the man in Antigua." MacGregor never mentioned him at all during our early meetings. When I later told him that Ramona had mentioned a big man in Antigua, he said he didn't mind talking about him, but didn't bring his name up again. When, in February 2016, they took Wright to Antigua for a pep talk, I e-mailed Matthews to ask if I could come, too, and he didn't reply. Wright, in a low moment, later asked me if I'd told MacGregor they were the ones who let the cat out of the bag about Ayre. I said it wasn't them: Ayre's name had first been mentioned to me by Matthews. The Antigua meeting was being arranged when I went out for dinner with Matthews, and he referred to Ayre freely without ever asking that it be off the record. MacGregor never went into detail about Ayre's involvement but both men's regular visits to Antigua made me wonder about the extent of the connection. Matthews, explicit as usual, always spoke about Ayre as if he was the *capo di tutti capi* of the entire affair, though I have no other evidence that Ayre was anything but an interested observer. Grippingly, nCrypt's only shareholder (one share worth £1) is nCrypt Holdings, registered in Antigua.

Like MacGregor, Calvin Ayre is Canadian. His father, a pig farmer, was convicted in 1987 of smuggling large amounts of Jamaican marijuana to Canada. When Calvin left college he went to work for a heart-valve manufacturer called Bicer Medical Systems and was later charged with insider trading, agreeing to a deal where he was fined $10,000 Canadian and barred from running a public company listed on the Vancouver Stock Exchange until 2016. "I clearly made some mistakes," Ayre told *The Vancouver Sun*, "but it was not a criminal issue and nobody got hurt from anything I did." Ayre later started a software development company intended to help offshore betting companies take online bets. He relocated to Costa Rica in 1996, where he worked with two online casinos, WinSports and GrandPrix. Unlike most bookmakers, Ayre would send checks directly, without using Western Union or an equivalent. He then set up Bodog, which would become the biggest name in the online gambling industry. (It's the company Matthews worked for after Centrebet.) Bodog was a huge success. In 2005, it handled more than $7 billion. Ayre appeared on the *Forbes* billionaires' list in 2006. In the same year, Bodog moved its global headquarters to Antigua.

The IRS had started following the company in 2003, and U.S. Customs and Immigration were also on his tail. A joint inquiry was started in 2006 and, in 2012, Ayre, along with two of the website's operators, was indicted on money-laundering charges. He entered no plea, but he maintains his innocence, seeing the indictment as "an abuse of the criminal justice system." In one profile of Ayre, we find him drinking coffee and paraphrasing Sun Tzu's *The Art of War*. "I've put a lot of energy into finding ways not to fight my enemies," he says. My researcher showed me this interview, then remembered a note from my first meeting with MacGregor, in which he, too, had quoted Sun Tzu. "You build your enemy a golden bridge to retreat over," MacGregor had said, drinking coffee. When he said this, I wasn't sure who the enemy was. The only person MacGregor had built a golden bridge for, so far as I knew, was Craig Wright.

At the Jermyn Street dinner, Matthews didn't tell me any of Ayre's history, referring to him simply as a great guy. "Do you know how many bitcoins Craig's got left of the original 1.1 million?" he asked later on. There are conflicting stories about the "Satoshi millions." Many people refer to a Satoshi-mined hoard that has never been spent, and the figure—always around a million—is the same one admitted to by Wright and Kleiman. The difference is that Wright says he spent a lot of his. This was what Matthews was getting at. "He told me last week," Matthews said, "and I've been having some sledgehammer conversations with Craig. I said to him: 'Time for straight answers on this one, my friend. How many coins are left under the control of the Seychelles trust? And don't tell me you don't know, because you're a grown man, and don't lie to me.' And his answer was one hundred thousand. I know that six hundred and fifty thousand was taken out to fund all the research and development stuff. And three hundred and fifty thousand is on Dave's hard drive. 'Why has Dave got three hundred and fifty thousand of your coins on his encrypted hard drive?' Because he gave them to him. They're Dave's. Those wallets are encrypted on his hard drive, with three or four keys to his trust. Now, why did Dave die in squalor?"

"Why?"

"Because bitcoins weren't worth that much when Dave died. They skyrocketed around that time and in the weeks thereafter. But he was a man of principle apparently and wouldn't spend those coins unless Craig told him to."

"And you don't think Dave mined coins himself?"

"Of course he did. No doubt. But how many? Who knows . . . We know they ran a business together based in Florida. They did stuff for contractors. We know that they lost money jointly in Liberty Reserve. And they would both have lost money in Mt. Gox."

Wright had told me he'd lost quite a bit when the bitcoin exchange Mt. Gox was hacked and then collapsed. He also referred, in a later e-mail, to information that was seeping from the collapsed Mt. Gox database, some of it linking him to Ulbricht. "The amount to a large wallet was me," Wright told me. I took him to mean that there was evidence of a bitcoin transaction between him and Ulbricht. He wouldn't explain further.

As I was paying the bill, Matthews reared up. "You know Craig has gone out and bought himself some cars? One hundred and eighty thousand dollars' worth of cars." (When I checked this with Wright he said the cars were leased.) "One of them stands out like the dog's balls in the proverbial moonlight, and this is from the man we're trying to keep fucking secret. How many custom BMW i8s are going around London? He's spending every fucking penny that we've paid him . . . Does he think this is just a game? You know, these guys have gone from being backyard scrappers and they've suddenly found themselves in a high-stakes poker game." Matthews said he wouldn't take any rubbish from the Wrights, and that they'd end up on a plane back to Australia and jail if they didn't fulfil their end of the bargain, to reveal Satoshi. "The people that I work with are capable of deciding this was a thirty-million-dollar bad decision and write it off," he said. I thought this a curiously revealing line, and wondered again just how he expected me to use such information.

"You haven't asked me why I'm doing this," Matthews said at the end of the evening. He worked his way around to an answer, but it wasn't an answer, just more questions. "Part of me," he said, "has asked over the past three or four months, why did I ever get involved in this? Why did Craig keep coming back to me? Why did he never shake out of my life? Why did he show me the Satoshi white paper in 2008? Why was he delivered back to me in 2015? I didn't go looking for it."

Satoshi Nakamoto is not really a man; he is a manifestation of public acclamation, an entity made by technology, and a myth. Old-fashioned journalism might bring you to him—or cause you to miss him altogether—but he was born of relationships that depend on concealment. A reporter was once a person who could rely on visible evidence, recordings, notes, statements of fact, and I gathered these assiduously, but this was a story that challenged the foundations on which reporting depends. I fought to uphold familiar standards of truth, and fought to discover new ways to uncover it in this underworld of companies with a vested interest in disclosing some things but not others, but it felt like the walls of virtual reality were forever pressing in on my notepad. It is standard practice in Silicon Valley for everyone, from bagel boy to research chief, to sign a nondisclosure agreement. This is because every company—Apple or Microsoft or Google or Facebook—has a mission not only to make money but to control the narrative of who they are. A writer requires determination if he is to write anything about that world that isn't paid for or manufactured by a company. There is nothing particularly underhand about this: they offer you big money up front and ask you to sign over your allegiance. But when you turn down this offer and they don't banish you from the court, your version of reality might end up clashing with theirs. This happened several times during the months I was working on the Craig Wright story. Wright himself never mentioned rights or agreements or privacy—until the very end, when he asked for two particular aspects of his private life not to be discussed—but when I went to Australia at the end of February to talk with Wright's family and friends, the nCrypt men began insisting I sign an NDA.

Why they hadn't asked me to sign one at the beginning I'll never know. I had roamed freely for three months, noting and recording, going to meetings and interviewing everyone, and only now did they want me to sign. Early on, MacGregor told me in an e-mail that he had advised Craig and Ramona to tell me "everything." He went on to express, on Wright's behalf, worries about how the material would be used. This was especially sensitive, I gathered, because of the government security work Wright had done. I replied that we would be judicious about what was published. MacGregor still wanted to discuss contractual issues, and I replied, on March 6, that I would have to see proof that Wright was Satoshi, and see it presented before his peers and selected journalists. MacGregor replied that the proof package was in train and that he didn't understand why I wouldn't sign. I replied on March 7 that I couldn't write the story, no matter how good my access, if there wasn't proof that Wright was Satoshi, and I was still waiting for evidence. "My commitment is clear," I wrote, "but the book turns to dust if we do not have unanswerable and generous proof." I insisted that I wouldn't sign any document and eventually MacGregor accepted this. We fell out over it, but I saw their point and I still do. Despite my refusal they continued, without binding agreements or legal constraints, to provide me with access to every meeting and every aspect of the story, which was set to change fast and in ways none of us could ever have prepared for. My story and nCrypt's deal seemed to be on the same track, aligned and friendly, but none of us discussed what would happen if the deal came unstuck.

Proof

When I asked Wright what kind of martial arts he did as a kid he gave the following answer: "I did a few, actually. I have studied in the Chinese forms Wing Chun, *Tánglángquán*, Kuo Shu, Duan Da, Zui Quan, and *lóng xíng mó qiáo*. I have also mastered Muay Thai, Kenpo, and taekwondo and Chito-ryu karate. I started with karate and ninjutsu." As with most things about him, it's not that it's not true, it just smells of self-doubt and a need not to hide anything positive about himself. It's the kind of truth-telling that expresses fear and gives rise to doubt, but it's not the same as a lie.

Wright's mother had told me about her son's long-standing habit of adding bits on to the truth, just to make it bigger. "When he was a teenager," she said, "he went into the back of a car on his bike. It threw him through the window of a parked car. That's where his scar comes from. His sister accompanied him to the hospital and he's telling the doctor that he's had his nose broken twenty or so times, and the doctor is saying 'You couldn't possibly have had it broken.' And Craig says: 'I sew myself up when I get injured.'" What his mother said connected with something I'd noticed. In what he said, he often went further than he needed to; further than he ought to have done. He appeared to start with the truth, and then, slowly, he would inflate his part until the whole story suddenly looked weak.

In the time since I'd last seen Matthews, he and MacGregor had been to Antigua with Wright and had agreed to a "proof strategy." I had been pushing hard for the proof, and Ramona had asked me several times what Wright could do to prove to me that he was Satoshi. MacGregor asked the same thing during a meeting I attended with him and the public relations firm they'd hired, the Outside Organisation. "It's not about proving it to me," I said. "It's about proving it—full stop. You just prove it for the whole world to see and then everybody goes home." The nCrypt guys, pointing out that they had always intended to set up a proof session, organized a series of events with the help of the PR company, intended to bring Satoshi into the open. Originally, the plan was for the London School of Economics to host a panel discussion about the evidence and the findings, but someone seems to have blabbed to the *Financial Times*, which ran an article on March 31. "After nearly four months of silence," the *FT* blogger Izabella Kaminska wrote, "and a bitcoin community mostly resigned to the notion that the story was an elaborate hoax—conditional approaches are being made to media and other institutions in connection to an upcoming 'big reveal' of Wright as Satoshi Nakamoto." Her source was clearly inside the project. "Wright will publicly perform a cryptographic miracle which proves his identity once and for all," she wrote. MacGregor was outraged, and the LSE was sacked from the project. But the first and biggest of these proofs was to involve Wright using Satoshi's private encryption keys in sessions with the most important members of the bitcoin community. Jon Matonis, the former head of the Bitcoin Foundation, agreed to take part. So did Gavin Andresen, one of the most respected bitcoin core developers, someone who had been there since its inception. These proof sessions would begin the denouement of this search for Satoshi.

Just before these sessions took place, in April, I asked Wright what had happened in Antigua. "We discussed the whole PR strategy," he said. "The truth thing is going to happen." He talked about Matonis and Andresen. "We're going to bring them in on reveal sessions in the next few weeks. I guess that's the way it has to be. Do I like it? No. But I haven't really been given a choice. I'm between a rock and a hard place because of whoever outed me last year." He said very clearly at a meeting with me that he would not sign with the key in public. We agreed that he would do it for me at home, signing with the private key from one of Satoshi's original blocks. He would do for me what he was going to do for Matonis and Andresen, and this would prove beyond doubt, he said, that he was Satoshi. We made a plan, then Wright asked me to come to his office so he could draw something for me on his whiteboard, a new time-lock encryption scheme he'd come up with. He wanted to add it to the list of patent applications. I didn't always know what he was talking about, but his expertise in certain areas was startling, and so were his obfuscations.

It was exactly 9:00 a.m. when I turned up at his house in South London, on one of those clear mornings when the planes leave trails in the sky. I knew his house by the BMW in the driveway, and I pressed the bell. He opened the door and a cloud of cologne came to meet me. In his study, there were three computers and seven screens. *Options, Futures and Other Derivatives* by John C. Hull was sitting on a gray sofa. There were rows of computing books and seven dead laptops stacked on top of a bookshelf. Even after all these months, Wright couldn't really do small talk, finding it hard to summon anything easy in himself. I asked him about his sofa and told him about a pain in my shoulder and he just said: "Very good." He made me a cup of tea and then beckoned me over to his main computer: it was time for him to prove to me that he was Satoshi. His manner was still that of a man who mildly resented having to prove anything. He smiled and pointed to the screen. "This is his wallet, which is open," he said. I saw a list of transactions with addresses specified. "The initial Genesis block was hard-coded," he said. "There are no conflicting Genesis blocks. If a piece of code crashed on this machine it would still start on another machine with the same Genesis block. Always." As I was looking at the screen in front of me and watching his hand move the mouse, lines from the Wikipedia entry on the blockchain came into my head: "The blockchain consists of blocks that hold time-stamped batches of recent valid transactions. Each block includes the hash of the prior block, linking the blocks together. The linked blocks form a chain, with each additional block reinforcing those before it."

"It can't be moved or changed?"

"No. It's hard-coded into the original program," he said.

Everything on his screen was time-stamped. I was looking at transactions from early January 2009. "I was officially canned from my job at BDO on January 3," he said. He told me he went to his house at Port Macquarie and settled down to do the final work to get the bitcoin software up and running. "The original definition was published by Satoshi Nakamoto in 2008 and implemented in the original source code of bitcoin published in 2009," the Wikipedia entry said. As he explained what was in front of me, he clicked through the sequential blocks, the transactions database that underlies bitcoin. He was looking at the very earliest ones and all included dates, amounts of bitcoin, and public keys. A long list of transactions showed incoming small amounts to Satoshi's wallet. "Lots of people send micropayments to me," he said. "They think so much of Satoshi that they want to burn their pennies."

"So these fans are sending tiny payments to that known address? It is the first generated and the first known address?"

"Yes. They're hoping I'll do something—out myself."

The address was 12c6DSiU4Rq3P4ZxziKxzrL5LmMBrzjrJX. I could see that people had left messages—"public notes"—for Satoshi: "Hey satoshi, change my life, send me some bitcoins!"; "God bless you, China"; "If you are reading this, please take some time to remember those who died 12 years ago today in the WTC attacks." "The bitcoin blockchain can be used as a trusted time-stamp for arbitrary messages," Wikipedia said.

If you scroll back to the very first transaction associated with this address—12c6DSiU4Rq3P4ZxziKxzrL5LmMBrzjrJX—you find that it is the first bitcoin transaction recorded. It was for 50 bitcoins and they remain unspent. Anyone can enter that bitcoin address into a search engine and inspect the history of transactions associated with it. "The Genesis block was hard-coded on January 3, 2009," Wright said to me, "and that was the first run. There was no previous block." (Under the heading "Previous Block," there is a line of 74 zeros.) "Then the code was reworked," he continued, "and fired up and the first address that was ever created from the hard-coded Genesis block—the first mined address—is the one I'm sending you a message from." He was about to use the original cryptographic key to sign a message to me and it was as if he were dropping a sugar lump into my tea. He typed the words "Here I am, Andrew," and rested his fingers. "This gives us that little block there," he said, before verifying the signature. He looked sheepish and resigned in his blue checked shirt. "Welcome to the bit I was hoping to bury," he said. He leaned back and I noticed a samurai sword by the desk.

I shook his hand. Then I stared at the screen and considered how strange it would be to live with a secret for seven years and then feel no relief when it finally came out. Perhaps it never felt like a professional secret; it felt like a part of his being, and now he was giving it up. "I want it in layman's terms," I said. "Explain what you just did."

"I just digitally signed a message using the first ever mined address on bitcoin."

If he had done what he appeared to have done, and what he said he'd done, then his claim to be Satoshi was strong. For a moment, the amassed unlikelihoods and dissemblings seemed circumstantial, and the case against him suddenly much more fanciful than the idea of him being the famously secret man who invented this protocol. An alternative Satoshi would have had to share his entire password hoard with him, and to have synchronized his "real world" timeline in order to be placed where Wright was placed and align with his e-mail existence and his expertise. It wasn't merely that Wright had been in the right place at the right time: he had been in the only place at the only time, and that time was stamped not only into the blockchain but into his correspondence and the experiences of those around him. He sat back in his large black chair and asked me if I wanted more tea. "I could have been working with Satoshi, I guess," he said, "who told me he was going to fire it up at this time and I had all my machines ready and just took over from him. But that would make me Satoshi anyway." He stared into the bank of screens and seemed nostalgic for a more ghostly self, and I asked him if it felt overwhelming.

"I don't care—whatever," he said. But of course he did care—care is what he did most. He was agitated through the whole process, mainly, I guessed, from an old cypherpunk embarrassment at having to bend to authority. He wasn't satisfied when he sat back in his chair, he was annoyed and already making his detractors' arguments for them. "They'll say I killed Satoshi and stole the keys. Having them doesn't prove I created them. Maybe it was a collaboration between me, Dave, Hal, and some random person. Maybe I compromised Hal's machine and stole everything and his family didn't know. Maybe, maybe, fucking maybe. All that bullshit. Those people don't believe in Occam's razor. I've seen Reddit. They want the most convoluted explanation. But they can say what they want; I've got nothing more to prove."

There is a message embedded in the Genesis block, a headline from *The Times* of January 3, 2009, the day the block was mined: "Chancellor on Brink of Second Bailout for Banks." I later asked Wright why he'd chosen that particular headline. "As you know, I am rather anti-central/reserve bank," he wrote to me. "I see them as the true cause of these issues and the bubbles and collapses. But the date was important as a time stamp. It means that I could not have been 'pre-mining' and gaming the system. The first iteration of the code was *finalized* on January 9, 2009. The run was started when I was at the farm in Macquarie later that week. It means that I cannot have been mining for months ahead and had collected a pre-mined set of solved hashes to game the system. I ran more than fifty machines, so the headline was a marker."

The question of proof in a story about computer science is a question for the birds. If you can't check the math, how can you be sure? I wrote to four Princeton and Stanford cryptocurrency experts during the preparation of this story and sent them some of Wright's white papers. These men, the authors of a textbook on bitcoin and blockchain technology, are obsessed with who Satoshi is, and obsessed with who he isn't. But they behave like visitors to a funhouse: they see distorting mirrors everywhere and hear distant laughter and weird music. Some of them did want to see the evidence, but they didn't want to be seen responding to it and I never heard from them again. And that is the kind of attitude that pervades the not entirely adult world of new inventions in computer science.

Another thing: when such people want to make a point, they often want to destroy those they disagree with. It's clear how paranoia-inducing it is to be constantly assaulted by people who hate you for thinking your thoughts. Geek culture in general is fantastically vitriolic: even an issue that seems pretty marginal to the rest of us—like the question of who might play Captain America's love interest—can easily spiral into death threats. In the world of cryptography, this has been a bar to invention and progress: developers are hung, drawn, and quartered every day on the Internet and they have to be unusually robust to take it. The question of how to take bitcoin forward has been riven with opposing views, and after Satoshi disappeared there was no central authority to lead the discussion or calm the waters. By increments, the task fell to Gavin Andresen, who was a Princeton graduate with experience in Silicon Valley. Andresen only gradually accepted the role of lead core bitcoin developer. This is not an official designation and he appears to have got none of the thanks and all the flak, but by general consensus he is the most levelheaded thinker in the bitcoin world. One insider said there was an irony in Andresen's situation that few people realized. "The word is that Satoshi passed the torch to Gavin before he retired in 2011," he said. "In fact, it was more like Satoshi threw the torch at Gavin and ran away leaving him holding it."

From time to time during those months, I wondered what if, in some brutally postmodern way, the true identity of Satoshi could never be fully ascertained? What if Wright had every single element necessary to prove himself, but somehow couldn't? Anonymity—or at least pseudonymity—is an essential part of the cryptographic world. I had a job on my hands—as did Mac-Gregor and Matthews, as would the core developers, as would the press—to establish the truth. Any narrative that is dependent on "outing" such secretive people is at the mercy of their basic hatred of being controlled or being known, and Wright was a spectacular example of this.

Andresen had been in touch with Satoshi in the early days and would have records of their conversations. He would presumably be able to ask Wright questions that only Satoshi could answer. In December 2015, after *Wired* published the story about Wright possibly being Satoshi, Andresen told the magazine he'd never heard of Craig Wright. But he began to believe in Wright once he started corresponding with him by e-mail in early April. At one point, Wright sent him two e-mails, one written in his own Craig Wright way, and another one, with essentially the same content, written as Satoshi would have written it. They discussed math and the history of the invention and the problems it had faced. Within a week, Andresen was sufficiently convinced to get on a plane to London. He was ready to see Wright sign a message to him using the original Satoshi cryptographic keys.

At this point, I began talking to Andresen. He told me he had written an e-mail to Wright before getting on the plane, asking for a little more of his backstory and for his thoughts on "the state of bitcoin in 2016." "He replied with a longish e-mail," Andresen told me, "on the state of bitcoin and why he decided to reveal his secret now, then followed up with a couple of in-progress research papers. The e-mail 'sounded like' the Satoshi I worked with, and the papers matched his academic, math-heavy voice, too."

Andresen crossed the Atlantic overnight, arriving at the Covent Garden Hotel at 11:00 a.m. on April 7. He went to his room—which had been booked, as had his flight, by nCrypt—and had two hours' sleep, after which MacGregor and Matthews ar-rived. "They gave me a lot of the background and explained their involvement," Andresen told me. When Wright turned up at the hotel, Andresen found it easy to talk to him, "although I was so jet-lagged," he wrote, "at one point I had to stop him from diving deep into a mathematical proof he'd worked out related to how blocks are validated in bitcoin."

Matthews had booked a conference room in the basement, and MacGregor could see that Wright was very emotional when he entered the room. I wasn't there, but I interviewed everyone who was in the room, and I can construct what happened. "He knew this was it," MacGregor said to me. "It's one thing to prove his identity to you and me, but the bitcoin community is something else. He knew that they would believe Gavin. He knew this was it—that he would have no plausible deniability after he'd talked to Gavin and shown him the keys." Before the meeting in the basement properly started, Andresen said to MacGregor—as he said to me—that some of the phrases Wright had used in their e-mail exchange had been "familiar" to him; he sounded like the Satoshi he had been in contact with before. Andresen asked MacGregor and Matthews a few questions about what nCrypt hoped to achieve with Wright's discoveries in the future. They didn't go into detail about the company's business plans, but they spoke about the future of bitcoin and alternative projects. Wright and Andresen quickly started scribbling on pieces of paper. Wright was using his big laptop to show his access to cer-tain addresses. It was a strange situation in all sorts of ways, and the main one, perhaps, was that Andresen, who had, once upon a time, left behind high-paying job opportunities to work on the bitcoin project for free, was possibly about to meet his hero. But he stuck to practical questions. He asked Wright about the trust and about his bitcoin holdings and what had happened to them.

MacGregor later told me that his first question after Matthews told him that Wright was Satoshi was "Well, why isn't he sitting on an island surrounded by piles of gold?"

Wright became quite relaxed. He explained what it had cost him to keep his companies alive and to pay for research and development, and the supercomputer. It was about 5:30 p.m. when he finally logged on to his laptop to do for Andresen what he had done for me in his office at home, sign a message with the key and have it verified. Andresen looked on. Wright had just used Satoshi's key. At that point, it seemed to some of those in the room that Andresen's body language had changed; he seemed slightly awed by the situation. He reached over to his bag and took out a brand-new USB stick and removed it from its wrapping. He took out his own laptop. "I need to test it on my computer," he said. He added that he was convinced, but that if people were going to ask him, he had to be able to say that he'd checked it independently. He pointed to Wright's laptop and said it could all have been preloaded on there, though he knew that was unlikely. But he had to check on his own computer and then they would be done. He said the key could be used on his laptop and saved to the memory stick and that Wright could keep it. But for his own peace of mind, and for due diligence, so that there wasn't a chance of fraud, he had to see it work on a computer that wasn't Wright's own.

Wright suddenly balked. He had just signed a message to Andresen from Satoshi, he said, and had demonstrated his complete familiarity with their correspondence, but, in his mind, what Andresen was now asking for was of a different order. "I had vowed," Wright told me, "never to show the key publicly and never to let it go. I trusted Andresen, but I couldn't do it." Wright got up from the table and started pacing. He had clearly believed he would be able to get through the proof session without this. In fact, he had said in my presence several times over the preceding months that he would never hand the key over to anyone or allow it to be copied or used on someone else's machine. "I do not want to categorically prove keys across machines," he wrote to me in an e-mail. To him, this would be to give Satoshi away and perhaps to dilute his own proclaimed connection to him. He went to a chair in the corner of the room and looked up at Andresen. "Maybe you and I could get to know each other better," he said.

Andresen just nodded his assent. "Like, trade more e-mails," Wright said, "and I can sign more messages to you."

At this point, Matthews's blood ran cold. "It was the only time during all the years that I thought: 'Jesus Christ, has he been spinning us the whole time?'" MacGregor, too, felt this was a very risky moment. He glanced at Matthews. There was no way he was going to let Andresen get back on the plane with *that* as a punctuation mark. They all felt Wright's behavior was ludicrous: he'd demonstrated that he was Satoshi and only had to let this be verified on Gavin's laptop. End of story. But Wright spoke to me later in a way that showed his old cypherpunk suspicion had reared its head: What if Gavin was a plant? What if the whole thing was a plot to rob him of Satoshi's keys and exploit him or deny him? Wright told me he felt strong-armed and that, for some reason, he couldn't let this thing go and remain himself.

Afterward, Andresen was sanguine. "The proof session took longer than expected," he told me. "I insisted that the verification happen on a computer that I was convinced hadn't been tampered with. And they"—Wright, Matthews, and MacGregor— "insisted that the signed message never touch a computer that could have been tampered with (the risk would be that the proof might leak out before the official announcement). So we waited a bit while an assistant went to a computer shop and got a brand-new laptop." The idea had been MacGregor's. He said the tension in the room was unbelievably high. Wright was refusing to do the one thing that would guarantee the success of his mission. He hadn't seen it coming, but Andresen wouldn't blindly trust Wright's hardware, and Wright wouldn't blindly trust Andresen's. The solution had to be a fresh computer straight out of the box. MacGregor called his assistant and gave her the task. "This is how you get your One," he said to her. (In his company the best score you could get in a staff appraisal was a One.) It was just before 6:00 p.m. on a Friday night and they needed a brand-new laptop in Covent Garden. The assistant got hold of one and rushed over from Oxford Circus to the hotel.

The new laptop was lifted out of the box. It took a while to connect it to the hotel's Wi-Fi and to load the basic software. "During all that time," Andresen told me, "it was obvious Craig was still, even then, deeply hoping his secret identity could remain secret. It was emotionally difficult for him to perform that cryptographic proof."

"It was tense and there was a bit of shouting. There were a few drops during the day about 'the evil businessman in the room,'" MacGregor said. "He stopped short of accusing Gavin of having a key-logger, but he clearly wasn't going to do it. He said he had trust issues, and he'd been attacked, and it had been so long, and he just couldn't bring himself over the line today, but they should keep talking. And Gavin was willing to do that. But we were like: 'No, no, no.' I remember what I said. I said, 'Look, Craig, you've just been alone for way too long. Gavin has dedicated a huge chunk of his life to what you invented. I think he has the right to see this. He is the friend you don't have: Stefan and I can't fill that role for you; Ramona can't. This is someone who really understands what you have been trying to do.'"

There were long silences. "He was on the edge," MacGregor said. Matthews was practically holding his breath. He didn't want to say too much out loud, so he texted MacGregor. The text said: "He should call Ramona." While MacGregor was out of the room Wright phoned his wife, and she said: "Do it." Everyone waited with bated breath as Wright used the new laptop to open the Satoshi wallet and set about signing a new message to Andresen. It failed. It wouldn't verify. He tried it again and again, until Andresen remembered that Wright hadn't typed "CSW" at the end of the message the way he had in the original, the one he was seeking to verify. When he put "CSW" at the end of his message to Gavin, it said: "Verified." Wright had demonstrated, on a brand-new laptop, that he held Satoshi's private key. They stood up and shook hands and Gavin thanked him for all he had done. There were tears in Wright's eyes. "His voice was breaking," MacGregor told me. "Gavin could see he was going through something." Both MacGregor and Matthews later said that Wright was turned inside out by the session. "I didn't want to just put him in a taxi," MacGregor said. Andresen was wiped out, so he went to get some fish and chips, and then headed to bed. "Craig broke down," MacGregor told me. "He said he thought he'd never have to do this. He said he never knew how to trust people in his life." Wright and Matthews and MacGregor went off to find a bottle of wine. "He was semi-apologizing for being a pain in the ass," MacGregor told me, "but I understood more than ever, at that point, how hard the whole thing was for him."

When I asked Andresen if he thought ending the Satoshi mystery might be good for the technology, he wasn't sure. "On one hand," he said, "having a mysterious founder is a great creation myth. People love a creation myth. Knowing the real story might make bitcoin less interesting to people. On the other hand, money is supposed to be boring—something that 'just works,' used by most people without understanding how or why it works. I'm excited to see how Craig contributes to making bitcoin work even better than it does today." I later met with Jon Matonis, who had been through his own proof session with Wright. He was equally impressed and relieved. He, too, believed the search for Satoshi had come to an end and he was looking forward to working with Wright, to seeing the patents and the new blockchain ideas. During our lunch in Notting Hill, Matonis suggested that this technology would change the world. One of the scientists at nCrypt said to me, "This isn't Bitcoin 2.0. This is something magnificent that will change who we are. This is Life 2.0," and Matonis agreed.

The idea was now to use the "proofs"—the gathered papers, the testimonies of the two bitcoin experts, the use of the keys, plus solid, document-heavy answers to every criticism previously made of Wright—and roll them out to selected members of the press on a certain day. I told MacGregor and Matthews I didn't want to go first with the story. I wanted to sit in on the interviews and proof sessions with the media organizations, and fold their reports, and the response to their reports, into my story.

Wright began to fade as we entered the proof sessions. He went from being a man with a clear picture of himself to being a fuzzy screen. He would e-mail me at all hours with a pressing sense of anxiety. He appeared to be losing it. Yet we all forged ahead to a conclusion that would be much more conclusive to him than anything he had ever expected, or could ever bear. He had signed up for it and was now faced with a full-frontal assault of cameras and lights. I had once asked him if he felt happy hiding in the Internet and he said yes, it was his home. On a good day it is the bright field that contains all souls but on a bad day it is the final darkness, where misery is gapingly exposed. I came to believe that Wright, this last year, was fighting for his soul on that plain, like Aeneas with his ships at his back and all hell in front of him, going down to an underworld where he might meet his own father. Wright told me, without demur, that his life had been an attempt to prove himself to his father. In the wee small hours, he seemed like a child whose fantasy had gone too far. And the fantasy was not that he is Satoshi. He may well be Satoshi. The fantasy was that he could live as Satoshi, and take his place among the great men, and forget the little boy who was slapped for losing at chess. Like Aeneas, he knew that his journey was as much ordeal as opportunity, and though, again like Aeneas, he had asked for it, the process was increasingly unendurable. "It is easy to descend into Avernus," the Sibyl in Seamus Heaney's translation of Book VI of the *Aeneid* tells Aeneas:

> Death's dark door stands open day and night.
> But to retrace your steps and get back to upper air,
> That is the task, that is the undertaking.
> Only a few have prevailed, sons of gods
> Whom Jupiter favoured, or heroes exalted to glory
> By their own worth.

The Reveal

By my last weeks with Craig Wright, I was in two minds about the moneymen, probably because I liked them. And while I wanted to assert my journalistic doubts—preserve my innocence, stand back from the parade—my wish for the reveal to turn out well was beginning to cajole my judgment. I was wise enough to say no to the world exclusive; I still wanted material I didn't have and I was convinced that the real proof of the pudding would be in the world's tasting of it. The Internet is great at crowdsourcing facts and establishing the accuracy of stories, and I had always felt this could be important. But in the meantime, I had to fight to give my doubts the oxygen they needed. The nCrypt boys said they understood—but did they? They appeared to have no Plan B if Wright couldn't prove to the world that he was who he said he was. People can start off by saying, "Write everything, warts and all," and end by saying: "I don't exist, maybe you shouldn't mention me." In a conversation with MacGregor at this point, I allowed for the possibility that I might give him a made-up name in the story. I said it because he seemed anxious, and because, as I told him at the time, he had brought the story to me and I meant him no harm—but this possibility depended on it being proved that Wright was Satoshi. Our discussion about using real names was inconclusive—during a later meeting at Berners Tavern, Matthews expressed the view that I should put their names in and make a final decision later—but the decision was really made by what the story became. The men in black seemed not to have prepared for any of that. They believed that only one big thing was going to happen: Craig Wright was going to emerge as Satoshi Nakamoto, the great mystery figure of the digital age, and the evidence would be "overwhelming." In the final week, as the men prepared the reveal, I found my independence slipping. No doubt about it: I felt like part of the team. I wanted to please MacGregor—pleasing people is my chief vice as a man and my main virtue as a reporter—but I could have told him my work so far might only be fieldwork. I wouldn't know how the story would turn out until it had turned out. Only in public relations is the story straight in advance.

In private, Wright was still saying he wouldn't "jump through hoops," but then I'd find him agreeing to do exactly what was asked of him. Only a few nights before the media appointments,

I was sitting with him in the Coach & Horses in Greek Street. The PR company, he told me, had asked if he wanted to go on TV, and he'd said there was no way in hell they'd get him in front of a TV camera. Yet it was all happening. I mentioned the fact that MacGregor, when I first met him, had spoken about all this ending with a TED talk in which Satoshi would be revealed.

"Rob always said 'eventually,'" Wright replied.

"But what does 'eventually' mean?" I asked.

"It originally meant '*if* you came out,'" Craig said.

The PR team, at MacGregor's behest, had been in touch with a number of journalists; the ones who were interested were from the BBC, *The Economist*, and *GQ*. The inclusion of *GQ* had irked Wright from the start (he sees himself as an academic), but the PR company, the Outside Organisation, had a connection there—their founder was a contributing editor—and said the magazine would love the story. But did the PR men explain to the editors there who was behind this project to out Satoshi, and who was paying their fee? I later asked them by e-mail and one of them replied: "It is not at all unusual to be instructed to represent an individual through an independent company. Our conversation with [*GQ*] and the other journalists was about the proposed story."

I e-mailed him again. "But did you tell them," I wrote, "that the outing of Satoshi was being done at the behest of a commercial company?" He didn't reply.

All the journalists had signed NDAs and embargoes. They would each be allowed a brief interview with Wright after he had demonstrated to them his use of the Satoshi key. These meetings would take place at the offices of the PR company in Tottenham Court Road on Monday, April 25, and Tuesday, April 26. I found all this a bit odd: Wright was being difficult, for sure, but the PR strategy was crazily old-fashioned. Everyone in the cryptography world knew that all Wright had to do was send an e-mail from the famous Satoshi e-mail address, alert people he was going to sign a message using Satoshi's keys, do so online, and move a single bitcoin from an early block, and the entire Internet would light up as if Coney Island were hosting the World's Fair. The piecemeal feeding of "proof" to these journalists was compelling but anachronistic. I supposed it was an attempt to get the story out of the world of crypto-gab and into the real media, but it was set up with an alarming sense of security paranoia. Wright could never have handled a celebration, but the journalists were being managed to an extent that might have raised more questions than it answered. I was just an observer, and was worried about Wright by then, and, though I believed in him, I felt distinctly that there was something missing and something wrong.

When I turned up at Starbucks in Tottenham Court Road, Wright, Ramona, and Matthews were already there. Wright was sulking a little. It had been decided that, as well as the demonstration, the journalists would be given a memory stick to take away with them, showing the signed Satoshi message. (Wright later told me the stuff he put on the sticks was fake. There wasn't anything on there they could understand, but it certainly bore no relation to any of Satoshi's keys.) Matthews was dressed smartly and wearing dark glasses, and Wright was wearing a gold tie and a business suit. Ramona sat beside him stroking his ear. "Let me know if you have trouble with the guys upstairs," Matthews said. He meant the PR guys. "Sometimes they forget their role." As usual, I found Matthews likable and easy to talk to, but he seemed not to appreciate the difference between his way of talking and the circus of manipulation surrounding us.

Rory Cellan-Jones, the BBC's technology correspondent, was led into a conference room with his producer, Priya Patel, and Mark Ward, a technology correspondent for the BBC News website.

Wright sat at his laptop, hardly looking up, and a screen on the wall showed what he was looking at. Matonis was in the room, and so was Matthews. Ramona had gone upstairs. Cellan-Jones was decent and professional, ready to get to the bottom of the story. He appeared to feel the tension, with Wright already behaving as if being asked questions was grossly humiliating and the questioner openly hostile. But Cellan-Jones was not hostile: if anything, he was mildly preconvinced, and just going about capturing the story for the layman.

"When I started out I asked myself what I'd need to see to know if someone who claimed to be Satoshi was Satoshi," Matonis said. "And you can break down three distinct lines of evidence: the cryptographic line, the social line, and the technical line. Obviously, the social and technical lines are going to be more subjective . . . On the cryptographic side, I'll explain what I witnessed personally and give you a lead up to what Craig's going to demonstrate this morning."

He then went into more detail about the cryptographic proof. "The Genesis block is block zero," Matonis said. "And you can't spend any of the blocks in that chain—which means that the ones that come after that (which are spendable) can be attributed to the creator of bitcoin."

"And what would they be called?" Cellan-Jones asked.

"In succession they'd be called block one, block two, etc. Now, this morning, Craig is going to demonstrate signing blocks one through nine. I personally witnessed the signing of blocks one and nine, so this is not going to be a transfer of bitcoins, it's going to involve a signing of a message, which he'll do with the private key and which will be verified by the public key. Are we clear on that?"

Eventually, Wright asked Cellan-Jones to give him a message.

"Um. 'Hi, historic message to the BBC.'" Wright typed the message and added a bit of commentary as he did so.

"This message will verify, but if I change a single digit, it won't," Wright said as he signed the message using block 9.

"This is the only key that we know is definitely owned by Satoshi, because it was used with Hal Finney," Matonis added.

"So," Cellan-Jones said, "just getting this clear in my mind. We've seen Craig use a private key known to have been used with Hal Finney. And we've seen it verified with the public key."

"Yes," Craig said. Then he proceeded to sign a message with the key associated with the first-ever mined bitcoin.

"Out of interest," Cellan-Jones said, "how many bitcoins do you have?"

"Well, that would be telling," Wright said.

"Do you still mine bitcoins?"

"Only for fun."

Wright then went into an aria about Sartre's speech when he turned down the Nobel Prize. He planned to use a hash function—which turns information into a unique set of letters and numbers—to attach Sartre's famous speech cryptographically to block 9, and then later verify it publicly on his blog. "He gave up the prize," Wright said, "because 'If I were to accept it, I'd become the institution.' I never wanted to sign Craig Wright as Satoshi," he continued. "I haven't done this because it's what I wanted, I just can't refuse it. Because I've got staff, I've got family. It's what I am and I'm not going to deny it because that's not the truth. So I'm choosing to sign Sartre because it's not my choice, I'm not choosing to come out, I've been thrust into it."

"In what way have you been forced into it?" Cellan-Jones asked, quite reasonably.

"I've got people mudslinging," Wright said. But that wasn't

true: he wasn't feeling forced because of what people said. He felt forced, or obliged, to come out because he'd signed the deal with nCrypt in June 2015. And he deepened the problem when Cellan-Jones asked him why he hadn't revealed himself before. "I liked to go to conferences, put out papers," he said. "I can't do that now. I can never just be Craig again."

He was asked whether he wanted to be the public face of bitcoin.

"I don't want to be the public face of anything." He paused and looked down. He then said that his blog would explain everything and help people to download the material and understand how the keys work.

"When does that go live?" Cellan-Jones asked.

"Monday or Tuesday."

"There will be people out there who will try desperately to prove this isn't the case. Are you confident that there are no chinks in your armor?"

"They'll say I stole keys, that I buried Satoshi in a ditch, they'll say all sorts of things."

The BBC planned to come back the next day with cameras. Then a man arrived from *The Economist*, Ludwig Siegele, a man in a gray suit. He was less immediately friendly but his questions were fine-grained. You could see he wasn't entirely comfortable with this very PR-managed way of outing Satoshi. Wright signed a message for Siegele using block 9, and had the private key verified by the computer. "I'm sorry," Siegele said, "but I'm still a little unsure what that proves."

"It proves I have the private keys," Wright said. "All the original private keys."

"OK, so. The first question that my readers are going to ask is: 'Why now?'"

Wright didn't hesitate. He was using his media training.

"I've tried to avoid media," he said, "but it's starting to affect other people. I'd prefer to stay quiet. Why now? I have staff, I have family . . . All the innuendo, the falsehoods." He had never suggested to me, in all our months of interviews, that he was outing himself because of media misrepresentation. I accepted it, though, when he said it to these journalists, imagining that perhaps he had realized that the tax office pressure was the real pressure in his life, the thing that forced the outing. I said this later to the nCrypt guys and they agreed.

"Why conceal your identity anyway?" Siegele asked.

"I don't want to be a public figure," Wright said. "I hope people don't listen to Craig Wright. They will look at the facts, not decide based on what Satoshi says."

That afternoon, I went to another appointment while Wright went off to Parsons Green to have his photograph taken for *GQ*. The next morning, at Starbucks again, Matthews was ridiculing the whole business with the photographs, and making fun of the magazine's original idea that he wear a mask in one photograph and rip it off in another. Matthews described what happened at the interview with the magazine's senior commissioning editor, Stuart McGurk. "It actually went quite well," Wright told me. "The journalist was nice, but he brought along this complete wanker of an 'expert.'"

The man they were talking about is a university lecturer in cryptology. McGurk brought him along to help verify the claims. "It was hilarious," Matthews said. "Craig threw the guy out." According to one witness, he'd questioned Wright quite forcefully about his understanding of public and private encryption keys. "He was totally in the guy's face at one point."

"He was telling me he was more qualified than I am," Wright said. "It became a nice interview but this guy was a complete idiot and I told him to get the fuck out." Matonis—who was there—said the scene was intense. I wasn't sure it was wise to greet dissenters and opponents, even ones who might be wrong, that way, but Wright was roundly applauded for doing so. I confess I felt it was wrong to tell journalists only half of the story, allowing them to misunderstand the reason he was suddenly coming out as Satoshi.

That day, the BBC came back. Wright was more irate than he had been the day before and less cooperative now that the camera crew was here. He felt he had done much more than he had ever wanted to and he said so, mainly under his breath. The cameraman set up the camera and then Cellan-Jones got into position. "So who are you? And what are you about to show me?" he asked.

"My name's Craig Wright, and I'm about to demonstrate the signing of a message with a key that is associated with the first transaction ever done on bitcoin—a transaction of ten bitcoin to Hal Finney."

"And who did that first transaction?"

"I did."

"And whose name is associated with that transaction?"

"The moniker is Satoshi Nakamoto."

"So you're going to show me that Satoshi Nakamoto is you?"

Craig looked bewildered for a second and hesitated. "Yes," he said.

"Are you confident that this will prove to the world that you are Satoshi?"

"It proves I have keys . . . other things we'll be releasing will help . . . Some people will believe and some people won't, and, to tell you the truth, I don't really care."

"But you can say, hand on heart, I am Satoshi Nakamoto?"

"I was the main part of it. Other people helped. At the end of the day, none of this would have happened without Dave Kleiman, without Hal Finney, and without those who took over—like Gavin and Mike."

"And this is going to have a huge effect on your life?"

"Unfortunately, yes."

Something changed in Wright in those few minutes. With these direct questions about Satoshi, his sense of himself—I don't know how else to put it—had come unstuck and he became noticeably uncomfortable. He said that he wanted to make the point that people should stop looking to him for answers.

"Make that point upstairs," Cellan-Jones said.

"Upstairs?"

"We're going to film a straightforward interview upstairs, without the computer."

Wright muttered something and stared into the depths of his computer as if he wanted to escape into it and never come out. "I just want the basis to be on the computer," he said.

The female producer interjected. "Because we haven't actually done that bit on camera yet," she said.

The PR executive came over, a little red in the face. "Can we do that bit upstairs?" he asked. "Are we all right to do the 'why now?' question upstairs? And we'll be done?"

"You know, I don't actually watch TV," Wright said.

The BBC left the room to scout out the location for the proper "sit-down" interview. Wright complained to me that he was being pushed. "I just didn't want a big facial shot of me," he said to the PR man. "I preferred to be behind the screen a little bit . . . I'm not against it, as long as I can hide behind the screen." The PR man said he didn't have to do anything he didn't want.

"I'm just doing the one question," Wright said. The PR man left the room.

"Does it feel completely against the grain of your nature to be asked 'Are you Satoshi?' like that?" I asked him.

"Yes."

"Is it a crude question to you?"

"Why does it matter, other than that you need someone to attack, someone to deify. I mean, fuck's sake. I'll do this. That's it. Fuck off. I can dance around saying 'please believe me.' But it's more than absurd, it's melting clocks on a landscape." At that point, the door opened and the PR consultant came in.

"Craig," he said, "we've explained to the BBC that you want to stay down here, and they're all making the point that this is the last thing you'll ever do . . ."

Craig started shaking and pushed his chair back. "No! No! No!" His face was pale. "You see this door," he said. "I don't want to hear another word. It's here, it's my way." Then he walked out and slammed the door, leaving me alone in the room with the PR boss.

"We're only doing our job," the boss said, with a shrug. Wright came back a second later and his microphone pack was trailing behind him.

"It's my way or I don't come back. OK? I'm not doing this for fucking PR stuff, I'm not doing this for anyone else. I don't give a fucking shit about what people say, I'd rather not do it. One word about it and I'll never come back. Not exaggeration. I will never enter this office again. I'll never answer an e-mail again, and I'll never talk to another PR person in my life again . . . Got it?"

"Yeah," the boss said.

"Thank you."

He went out and I was alone with Wright again. "They've already pushed me," he said. "I'm already beyond where I want to be: I'm already doing a TV thing. And everything is always:

'Let's take it a little bit further, a little bit further.' Which bit of 'Go away' don't they get?"

I asked him if Kleiman would have handled it better. "Better than I do," he said. "He would still have told them to fuck off. But in a nicer way. Hal would have done it far better."

"What do you think they're talking about up there?" I asked.

"The fact that I don't want to jump through their fucking bloody crap. 'This man has a big credibility gap he's got to overcome, I'm open to being convinced he's Satoshi but . . .'"

The BBC came back downstairs to ask their "one question" and, naturally, Cellan-Jones asked more than one. In the panicked and hostile mood Wright was in, he needed scapegoats, and the PR weren't meat enough and Matthews was too much the boss. So he scapegoated the BBC, saying, as soon as they left the room, that they had broken their "contract" with him, that they were liars. "I'll never do any television interviews again in my life," he said. "Never." And as he said it, I was imagining him with Fox News or the rottweiler interviewers. "The whole thing was just an attempt to expose me as being something I'm not," he said.

"That was actually a pretty softball interview, Craig," I said. "You can't blame them for turning up and asking for proof."

"Are you talking about proof or evidence? You're conflating the two. They're not the same and that's one of the things I'm saying. I gave them proof. They want more."

Wright was happy to lecture you day and night about algorithms, but he wouldn't name names, and he struggled to provide real-world evidence of Satoshi's footprints. The more I thought about it, the more I realized something was wrong, for him, with the footprints analogy, because if Satoshi was only one man he would have only one set of prints. The Satoshi who existed online could be any number of people. But there was something revealing about his treatment of the BBC—something not very nice in his attitude to people who make it their business to ask straight questions—and the handling of the proof sessions made it clear how much of a danger he was to his own credibility. A month later, when I asked Cellan-Jones if the PR company had ever explained to him that there was a commercial company behind the outing of Satoshi, he said he had never been given that information, "just that they were representing the man who was Satoshi."

Life Rights

At 7:51 a.m. on Monday, May 2, 2016, all was quiet on the Twitter front. Well, not quiet, but the names Satoshi Nakamoto and Craig Wright were nowhere to be seen. This was the day of reckoning, the day the embargo would lift and the media outlets could run their pieces and name Satoshi. At 7:55, *Game of Thrones* was trending and so was Gerry Adams, for allegedly using the word "nigger." Also trending was a wildfire in Fort McMurray in Canada and a bombing in West Bengal. There's a strange feeling of supreme calm before a storm breaks. At 8:00, Wright posted a blog containing the supposed hash of the Sartre speech and various postings about himself as Satoshi. At the same moment, Gavin Andresen posted a message to his blog. Title: "Satoshi." "I believe Craig Steven Wright is the person who invented Bitcoin," it began.

> I was flown to London to meet Dr. Wright a couple of weeks ago, after an initial email conversation convinced me that there was a very good chance he was the same person I'd communicated with in 2010 and early 2011. After spending time with him I am convinced beyond a reasonable doubt: Craig Wright is Satoshi.

Part of that time was spent on a careful cryptographic verification of messages signed with keys that only Satoshi should possess. But even before I witnessed the keys signed and then verified on a clean computer that could not have been tampered with, I was reasonably certain I was sitting next to the Father of Bitcoin.

During our meeting, I saw the brilliant, opinionated, focused, generous—and privacy-seeking—person that matches the Satoshi I worked with six years ago. And he cleared up a lot of mysteries, including why he disappeared when he did and what he's been busy with since 2011. But I'm going to respect Dr. Wright's privacy, and let him decide how much of that story he shares with the world.

We love to create heroes—but also seem to love hating them if they don't live up to some unattainable ideal. It would be better if Satoshi Nakamoto was the codename for an NSA project, or an artificial intelligence sent from the future to advance our primitive money. He is not, he is an imperfect human being just like the rest of us. I hope he manages to mostly ignore the storm that his announcement will create, and keep doing what he loves—learning and research and innovating.

I am very happy to be able to say I shook his hand and thanked him for giving Bitcoin to the world.

Also at 8:00 a.m., with the embargo lifted, the first tweet appeared, from Rory Cellan-Jones: "Craig Wright tells BBC I am bitcoin inventor Satoshi Nakamoto, publishes evidence backing his claim." One minute later, a tweet appeared from @CalvinAyre, naming Craig Wright as the proven Satoshi. *The Economist* went one minute later, with a link to Ludwig Siegele's open-minded piece asking for more and better evidence. At 8:09 Radio 4's *Today* program broadcast Cellan-Jones's report: "I'm about to demonstrate the signing of a message with a key that is associated with the first transaction ever done on bitcoin." The report was brief and quoted Wright once. It said Wright hoped to disappear and that that would be difficult. They played the part of the interview where Wright said he was part of the group behind Satoshi.

"He sounds plausible," Justin Webb, the presenter, said, laughing. Then they played part of the interview with Matonis, who said he was "one hundred percent convinced."

"Why should people be excited by this?"

"I put it on the level of the Gutenberg printing press," Matonis said.

"Quite a lot of people are saying that this is as important as the Internet," Cellan-Jones reported, "and that this man—if he is the man—should be celebrated like Tim Berners-Lee."

"Craig Wright has just outed himself as the leader of the Satoshi Nakamoto team," the bitcoin insider Ian Grigg wrote on his blog:

> Sometime in summer of 2015 the secret started to spread, and the writing was on the wall. An extortionist and a hacker started attacking, perhaps together, perhaps apart; to add to the woes, Dr. Wright and his companies were engaged in a long harsh bitter battle with the Australian Tax Office . . . Since then, the team has been more or less in hiding, guarded, at great expense and at some fear . . . Satoshi Nakamoto dies with this moment. Satoshi was more than a name, it was a concept, a secret, a team, a vision. Now Satoshi lives on in a new form— changed. Much of the secret is gone, but the vision is still there. Satoshi Nakamoto is dead, long live Satoshi. Yet, a warning to all. Satoshi was a vision, but Craig is a man. The two are not equal, not equivalent, not even close . . . It is true that Craig is

the larger part of the genius behind the team, but he could not have done it alone.

Over the following two hours the words "Craig Wright" were typed into search engines tens of thousands of times, and the Reddit forums and the cryptocurrency community got to work. Meanwhile, I was being copied into the e-mails sent from the PR company to nCrypt and the Wrights. It issued a press release spreading the news to less favored outlets. "Wright's decision to go public follows a series of misleading statements that are circulating and which he seeks to set straight," the release said. "Wright has also launched a blog, with a vision to create a forum about bitcoin, which dispels myths and helps to unleash its full potential. He will create a space to provide developers and producers with the real facts about the technology so as to encourage the widespread use of bitcoin and the blockchain."

"Great start!" the top PR man wrote to the group at 9:31 a.m.

"Ta. All going well," Wright wrote just before ten.

"All going to plan," the second PR man echoed a few minutes later.

"Right on course so far," the first PR man wrote at 10:13. And that was the last of the good news to come from the world of public relations.

By midday the blog was receiving the wrong sort of attention. A number of researchers had studied what Wright had written and noticed that the explanation was fudged—worse than fudged, it was faked. Something that he said was signed with the Satoshi key had, in fact, been cut and pasted from an old, publicly available signature associated with Nakamoto. It was astonishing and the buzz quickly grew fierce. In all those months, Wright had appeared to pass all the tests, or avoid them, but what was this if not an unequivocal attempt to defraud? All those hours in secret apartments scrolled through my head. There had always been something missing, something he hadn't wanted to show. But was that because he wouldn't, or because he couldn't? The thought that he would fake proof so publicly and so coarsely was hard to comprehend. Yet here was the smoking gun. He sent me an e-mail. "They changed my blog post," he wrote. "It will be back as I wanted. But first I need to negotiate with Stefan." And I replied: "How did they change it?"

I thought he was lying. He had lied before, but to lie so transparently and so publicly made me think he had lost his mind. There was no way to square such actions with his wish to have no publicity. He had faked his own proof, and now he was being ripped apart on the Internet. I briefly wondered if he might be enjoying the cries of execration, but how could he do that to Andresen and Matonis? Suddenly his opponents seemed wiser and greater in number. That day, I began to see that Wright's action might be consistent with something deeper in his character. He never wanted to come out and when it came to it he flunked his own paternity test. But I had a feeling that he was too close to the invention to be a simple hoaxer.

"I will explain why I think he's probably not Satoshi," said Vitalik Buterin, a big wheel in the cryptocurrency scene, speaking at Consensus, a bitcoin conference in New York. A friend of mine was there. He said that men had started the day high-fiving and shouting "Satoshi, baby," but that as the long day closed, his name became the punch line of every joke. Core developers and others were calling for him to sign something new and in public right away, using the Genesis block, which is unquestionably Nakamoto's. One of them, Peter Todd, was quoted by *Forbes*: "All Wright needs to do, says Todd, is to provide a signature on the message 'Craig Wright is Satoshi Nakamoto' signed by a key known to be Satoshi's. 'This is *really* easy to do . . . if you're actually Satoshi. Also, you'll know sufficient proof has been provided when it actually happens, because cryptographers will be convinced.'"

That was the strangest element of all: Wright must have known, having been a cryptographer all his adult life, that his fraud would be spotted immediately. But when I asked him about it he said it wasn't a fraud, it was a mistake. "I cut and pasted something just for the time being but knew I would change it later," he said. "But then it went up." That rang hollow to me, the words of a falling man. He intentionally faked it. I believed at that point that he had misled his colleagues and tried to get out of being Satoshi, which isn't necessarily the same thing as not being him. "I can't think of a more convoluted way to go about claiming one is Satoshi than what Craig Wright has done so far," Jerry Brito, the executive director of Coin Center, a think tank, told *The Daily Beast*. "He's provided no cryptographic evidence verifiable by the public, and many of his answers sound plain fishy." Emin Gün Sirer, a Cornell professor who had criticized Wright before, referred to Wright's "meta-modernist play."

The next day, I turned up at MacGregor's office and found him sitting with Matthews in a dark meeting room. They were hunched over the desk, exhausted and shell-shocked. When I asked them what had happened MacGregor shook his head. It was the first time in six months I'd heard him sounding incoherent. "Craig happened," he said. "He got cute with the math. He has been trying to get consent from the trustees to get the private keys . . . But he wasn't allowed access to coin or to do anything other than that. So what he was trying to do was re-sign a message . . ." Matthews butted in, saying Wright never had authorization from the trust to use the key publicly or let anyone take it away.

"Why didn't he just say that?" I asked.

"You tell me," Matthews said. MacGregor went on to explain how a signed message can be used nefariously by people with enough computing power. He said the trustees didn't want anyone analyzing those blocks. I'm not sure if he was grasping at straws, but what he said didn't explain the suddenness or the fraudulence of what Wright had done. MacGregor said that he and Matthews had since been with Wright and indicated that the encounter had been shouty and ugly. But he said it was OK now. "We have verbal consent from the trustees to move coin, and we're just waiting on the written consent."

MacGregor and Matthews had been in the meeting room for hours trying to work everything out. They thought it could all still be kept on track. MacGregor was writing new blog posts for Wright. He asked for my help with one of them and I explained that I had now to distance myself from the whole thing. I had got too close. MacGregor said they were going to "flood the blog with evidence" and get Wright to "move" some of the Satoshi bitcoin, to transfer it to someone else in a way that only someone in possession of Satoshi's private keys could do. Andresen had agreed to be on the other end of the coin transaction.

"Craig is being mauled out there," I said.

Rob removed his glasses. "The first meeting we had with him yesterday ended with: 'You're fired. Buy a ticket to Sydney. You fucked us. Good luck with the ATO.'"

"He didn't sleep last night," Matthews said. "He looks fucking terrible."

"He risks destroying his entire reputation."

"His and ours," MacGregor said. "I've been taking meetings with investment bankers for the last two months. I've pulled every string I know to get meetings with Google and Uber. If he goes down in flames, I'll go down with him. I mean, he's fucked me. Millions of dollars out of my pocket, nine months out of my life. But what we have now is a very pliant Craig Wright. We're going to drag this back from the brink."

"It's a big task, Rob," I said.

"We finally beat him to a pulp today. No more decisions. This is what we're going to do, because he knew the next move was pack your toothbrush and get on a plane and good luck in Australia." MacGregor told me he'd started Monday morning on an unbelievable high. "I can't believe we kept all the puppies in the box this whole time," he'd thought to himself. "Nobody broke embargo, holy shit this is going to work. And then . . ."

We spoke about Wright's possible lies. I said that all through these proof sessions, he'd acted like this was the last thing he ever wanted.

"That's not true," MacGregor said. "He freaking loves it. Why was I so certain he'd do that BBC interview the next day? It's adoration. He wants this more than we want this, but he wants to come out of this looking like he got dragged into it." He told me if everything had gone to plan, the groundwork was laid for selling the patents. It was a really big deal. He said Ramona had said that if Wright doesn't come out you still have this really smart guy who has made all these patents, who knows all about bitcoin. "Yeah," MacGregor said. "You and five hundred other guys who have called today." I shook their hands and wished them luck, thinking I would probably never see the men in black again. And as I descended in the elevator, I thought I would miss their brio and their belief, despite everything.

Craig was lost in some labyrinth of his own making, or mostly of his own making. He didn't want to be Satoshi. And he didn't want to be Craig. And he didn't want to be a letdown. And yet the message boards lit up and the walls closed in. Over the next twenty-four hours, he agreed to move Satoshi's coin and his blog advertised the fact. It said, "Extraordinary claims require extraordinary proof," and he was set to provide it.

On Wednesday, May 4, Matthews was at Wright's house organizing the movement of coin. The new (and final) proof session was intended to blow away the doubts created by the first. Many commentators felt it was too late, that Wright was beyond the pale, but Matthews and MacGregor had agreed with Andresen that the movement of coin, to Andresen and also to Cellan-Jones at the BBC, would undo the damage. Wright spoke to Andresen on the phone from his house—Andresen was in New York—and told him he was worried about a security flaw in the early blockchain, a problem in the way those first blocks were constructed that would make it dangerous for him to move coin, exposing him to exploitation or theft. My sources say that Andresen understood the problem and confirmed that it was all right, it had been fixed. But Wright continued to worry and was showing great reluctance about offering the final proof. Then he left the room abruptly and didn't come back.

The next day, he sent me an e-mail. It linked to an article headlined "UK Law Enforcement Sources Hint at Impending Craig Wright Arrest." The article suggested that the father of bitcoin might be liable, under the Terrorism Act, for the actions of people who used bitcoin to buy weapons. Under the link, Wright had written an explanation: "I walk from 1 billion or I go to jail. I never wanted to be out, but if I prove it, they destroy me and my family. I am the source of terrorist funds as bitcoin creator or I am a fraud to the world. At least a fraud is able to see his family. There is nothing I can do." I am still not sure if Wright was faking his fear of the FBI. He'd certainly never mentioned them to me before that day, and there seemed little evidence that they were seeking to arrest him. Indeed they never have. The truth, as usual with such men, seemed to be closer to home: he was a mass of paranoia that went all the way back to the fundamentals of his life. His online existence had stripped him bare and he was no longer sure if he was anybody at all. I believe that self-sabotage is in his nature, as it is in Julian Assange's nature, exacerbated by an ego that would sooner die than admit to being wrong. Wright never for a second admitted to me that he'd been caught out. He simply wallowed in the bad decisions he had made and said it was beyond his power to correct them. He was Satoshi, he said, but even he couldn't prove it the way people wanted it proved.

He knew his dream was over. He was devastated. He was the runner who failed twenty yards short of the finishing tape, the man who froze at the moment of truth and started walking backward. He said he feared prosecution on the one hand and humiliation on the other. The borstal boy in Alan Sillitoe's "The Loneliness of the Long-Distance Runner" comes from a family who make much of running, "especially running away from the police." He hates being understood, feels authority is there only to grind you down, and holds on to his essential privacy, knowing "they can't make an X-ray of our guts to find out what we're telling ourselves." The boy lives on his own terms, which means not faking it for power, even when the pressure is high and the rewards are obvious. So he refuses to win. Representing the borstal in a championship race he is well ahead of the other runners, but he stops, and lets them pass, and at the end jogs up to the tape: "I got to the rope," Sillitoe writes, "and collapsed, with a murderous-sounding roar going up through my ears while I was still on the wrong side of it." In another e-mail that day Wright wrote: "Andrew, I don't know what I can say. If I was to do the proof and save myself, I damn myself." That afternoon, he closed down the blog—the one that was intended to lead cryptocurrency fans into a new era—but left a final posting:

I'm sorry. I believed that I could do this. I believed that I could put the years of anonymity and hiding behind me. But, as the events of this week unfolded and I prepared to publish the proof of access to the earliest keys, I broke. I do not have the courage. I cannot. When the rumours began, my qualifications and character were attacked. When those allegations were proven false, new allegations have already begun. I know now that I am not strong enough for this. I know that this weakness will cause great damage to those that have supported me, and particularly to Jon Matonis and Gavin Andresen. I can only hope that their honour and credibility is not irreparably tainted by my actions. They were not deceived, but I know that the world will never believe that now. I can only say I'm sorry. And goodbye.

The next morning I drove through the traffic to a London suburb. It was early in the day and the high streets were empty, the happy boutiques, the delis, and the wicker-and-candle dens where people come to improve their mood or do something about their lifestyle. Craig and Ramona were sitting in the corner of a popular café. They were holding hands and staring at the table. He was wearing his Billabong T-shirt—I remembered it from his description of the clothes he'd bought in Auckland when he began his long-distance run last December. He looked as he'd looked the first night I met him in Mayfair: unshaven, unslept, the scar on his face more livid, his pupils like pinpricks and his breathing heavy. He wasn't just white, he was empty-looking, and his hands were trembling. Ramona was crying. The light of the café seemed too much for the darkness enclosing them. I went to shake his hand but we hugged instead, and it was like embracing a drowning man. He hadn't really slept since Monday and this was Friday. He wasn't drinking his latte; he made clouds on the spoon, and stared.

"Well, it was worth about a billion dollars to them," he said. Ramona talked about jail and I asked if they were afraid of being prosecuted.

"They say it'll never happen," she said. "Of course it will . . . So how can he? How can he?" He spoke of men he knew who had sold bitcoin and had been prosecuted for money-laundering and said they might try to do that to him. "It was always a present danger," Ramona said. MacGregor, Wright alleged, had always had a plan to move him if necessary to Manila or Antigua if it looked like he might be arrested.

"It's always been incremental," Wright said. "One step, one step, and nobody realizes that eventually that takes you over a precipice."

"That's the thing," Ramona said. "Your happiness doesn't count at all. But now we're stuck. You come out—you go to jail. You don't come out—you're a fraud. It's got to the point where it's almost better if he's a fraud."

"So what happened on Monday," I asked, "when it came to writing that blog?"

"I gave them the wrong thing," he said. "Then they changed it. Then I didn't correct it because I was so angry. Which was stupid. I put up the wrong one. No one wants SN. I will never be SN. I'm not personable. You can lock me in a room and I'll write papers, I'll never be personable."

Ramona was crying. "They could take us down," she said. "They could really take you down if they want to."

They spoke about moneymaking ventures Wright was involved in a long time ago. Wright alleged Matthews knew about these activities, which was true, because Matthews had mentioned them to me.

"I just couldn't do things anymore," he said. "That's all."

They wanted to talk about the trust, but they didn't really

explain it. He said it was to hide the bitcoin. "It's not meant to be spent," he said. "Too many problems."

. "It's also a guarantee that you can't flood the market," Ramona said. "That we can't use it to pay the bills, no matter how desperate things get." When I asked who the trustees were they went quiet.

Ramona began to worry about my story. She tried to strong-arm me. She began to tell me what I should say and what I shouldn't say and how I should hide from MacGregor and Matthews the comments she and Wright had made about them. "I want to write the truth," I said.

She said I knew too much. She said that Craig would go to jail or harm himself if I told everything I knew. I was stunned. There were many things that were said to me by every party in this story that I would choose not to print. Not only things they said about one another, but business arrangements and unsubstantiated allegations about the past, and things I knew in the present. But I had been recording this as a documentary from the start, as I'd said I would when we met at Claridge's in December. Now I was being told that my material was too hot and my story posed a threat.

Wright suddenly got very upset. His face crumpled and he put his head in his hands. "And the Brits have their equivalent of Guantánamo Bay as well," he said. "I'll never write, I'll never see anyone. I'll be in a little room. I won't even have a pen and paper. I won't see my wife again. I'll never see . . ." He sobbed and was inconsolable. "I'll never write again."

"They won't do that," Ramona said. I suggested they might get a lawyer to advise them on the possible threats they faced. Ramona said it was too expensive. She said the bills would run into the millions. Wright talked about Ian Grigg and others who'd "outed" him last year by nominating him for various awards. Satoshi was nominated for a Nobel Prize and a Turing Prize. Wright told me that people in the bitcoin community wanted him to come out and receive recognition. He said it had never been in his interest to come out, but in other people's interest. "I don't care if people like my work," he said. "I just have to *do* my work. That's the only thing that'll keep me sane."

"I would like that his reputation gets redeemed but I don't know if that's possible," Ramona told me. "This is what I propose, if you can do it, you do it, if you can't, it's up to you. If [you say] he didn't choose to come out . . . then the company gets put in the spotlight. If you say you know he is Satoshi then we're in trouble. If you say you have your doubts then he looks like a fool."

I'm sure I looked at her disbelievingly. "You're basically saying that every version of the truth of this story is untellable."

"But if you say it, Andrew . . ."

"If you were sure that this could never be said in the end, then you should never have allowed it to happen."

"It was one step, then one step . . ." Wright said, again.

"And you let a writer into your life?" I said.

"Do you know how much this meant to me?" Wright said. "The company. The people. To be doing that. To get all these papers out. To be in that position. It's my idea of heaven, but the cost is hell."

"If we didn't cooperate with you," Ramona said, "they'd stop . . ."

I reminded them that every time I'd tried to walk away from this story—like when they tried to make me sign an NDA—she'd begged me to come back. I told them that full disclosure was much less damaging than any other option. Naturally enough, that was my view.

"No one wants to believe me," Wright said.

"And I think that's great," Ramona said. "It's great that no one wants to believe you."

Wright said he'd filed all these patents and they were all from him, "not just Dave."

"What do you mean," I asked, "'not just Dave'?"

"I mean I wrote those patents," he said. "It means I knew all this shit."

"Have you been able to talk to Matonis or Andresen?" I asked.

"No," Ramona said. "I don't know if they'll even talk to us."

"I think you should have some crisis management advice."

"From who?"

"From a therapist."

"We don't have time for that," she said.

I walked home with them and he slumped on a sofa, looking wan, gone. "His mental health is fucked," she said to me when he was out of the room. "If he goes to jail, he'll kill himself. I can't leave him alone."

When he returned he seemed almost paler than before. "This is all because I wrote code," Wright said. "Not because I blew up something, because I wrote code."

"Just out of interest," I said. "If you are a fraud . . . How hard a fraud would it have been to perpetrate?"

"It would be the best one in human history," Craig said. "It'd be Ronnie Biggs on steroids times a million. I invented a new form of money. Who has ever had anything to do with money that wasn't to do with government? Who has ever really succeeded?"

"You mean it's a thankless task?"

"It's always Prometheus," he said.

This was a story in which everybody wanted their story told, then untold, then hidden, back in the vaults. It seemed like a very new story, but, in fact, it was a very old one, a story of metamorphosis, and of Prometheus unbound. Craig Wright proved cryptographically that he had Satoshi's keys, his e-mails seemed to show his involvement, his science extrapolated from the technology of the blockchain, and he spent a full year engaged in a business plan to reveal it all. But, when it came to it, he behaved like a fraud, he shape-shifted and he dissolved.

I began to wonder whether Craig Wright might be a man who had never known who he was, a missing person, constantly in discussion with some inner lost self, unable to bear the conditions that forced him to say definitively who he was. Some people, it could be said, *really* aren't anyone, in the sense that the complications of being themselves have wiped them out. The Internet eats its own ciphers, and Wright is one of them. He might have sabotaged his own proof or simply flunked the paternity test because he isn't the right man, but his own doubts about himself are the real drama. He was sick, he was brilliant, he was manipulative—but much of what he said was true. And as I drove away that morning, it was the sickness that seemed predominant. Wright was a clever man who had gone to the very end of himself to prove who he wasn't. "We are all Satoshi now" became a tagline for bitcoin's early fans. And in the end we all are Satoshi, and we'll begin to accept it as paper currency starts to look stale, and our minds merge with our computers. There are new networks up ahead that will have grown from the seed Satoshi planted, and it was odd, after all my travels, to believe that the only man who wanted to opt out of being Satoshi was Craig Wright. A week after his "proof sessions" with the BBC and others, he was in complete disgrace, his corner office at nCrypt had been emptied, and his leather sofas had disappeared, removed from the building with the signed Muhammad Ali picture and the rest of his stuff. Without ceremony, the best room in the office became a conference room and his name was spoken in whispers.

My last meeting with MacGregor and Matthews was a time of conjecture and anger, devastation and apology. They felt Wright had perjured himself, and for no good reason. He had never admitted to problems with the trust, problems that would make the Satoshi reveal very difficult for him. They still believe, as do Andresen and Matonis, that he is Satoshi. To them, there is just too much evidence to accept Wright's late attempt to cloak himself in deniability. But no matter. He was now fired, they said, and the deal with Google was off. "He put a gun to our head and pulled the trigger," MacGregor told me. "The world is still going to think we got fooled, but I know the facts. He has the keys." There was a moment in our meeting when I realized this had gone all the way to the bone with MacGregor. He said he never wanted to see Wright again. "This was supposed to be so noble," he said, "and it became so dark." Matthews told me that Wright's office, his house, his job, his work visa, everything, was set to go. They had spent as much as $15 million and maybe lost a billion. MacGregor said the PR company would never deal with him again, and there were investment bankers who weren't picking up his calls. A way would be found, however, to continue developing the blockchain technology. The company would go on. MacGregor shook his head. The whole thing was unfathomable. It was baffling. For no obvious reason Wright had found a way to disappear back into the shadows.

Coda

Wright seemed to miss me. He wanted to meet. It was a few weeks after the abortive "reveal," and I saw when I got to Patisserie Valerie that he was happy again and ready to take on the world. "It was unfair of me to request you not to publish certain things about our situation," Ramona had written to me in an e-mail. "As you said, you have a debt to the truth, and that is as it should be." And yet, as we all know, the truth has more faces than the town clock.

Wright told me in Patisserie Valerie that he felt free again. He had lost a third share in a billion dollars but he felt unburdened. He was sorry to have let good people down but now he could work in peace. Sherlock Holmes's central precept came into my mind: "When you have eliminated the impossible, whatever remains, however improbable, must be the truth."

"Do you want to know what I think?" I said to him after he told me again that all would be well from now on.

"Yes."

"What if you were thirty percent Satoshi. You were there at its formation and you were part of a brilliant group. You coded and you synthesized other people's work and you shared in the encryption keys. Then, sometime in the last year, you upgraded yourself to eighty or ninety percent. You were already a lot more Satoshi than anybody else has been hitherto, but the deal, in your eyes, required you to be more and in the end you couldn't carry that off."

"No," he said. And he flew off on a tangent about elliptical curves and the nature of the blockchain and how he never wanted to be a deity. I turned off my recording head at that point and stared through him.

Outside the café, he shook my hand. I knew I would never see him again. For six months we had allowed each other to think we were friends—subjects need storytellers, and storytellers need subjects. There had been a time when he'd imagined that I could free him from his fictions and build him a new story in reality. I was a willing stenographer, thinking Wright was something perhaps bigger than Satoshi. He was the Internet's habit of self-dramatization and self-concealment all at once; its new sort of persona. What he actually did may never be known. Either he's one of the greatest computer scientists of his generation or he's a reckless opportunist, or he's both. We can't be sure. But there he was, standing in Old Compton Street in the pouring rain, saying sorry. When I left him, he was still talking, looking for a fresh incarnation and introducing his next move. He was standing under an umbrella, a smart phone buzzing in his hand, and I touched his arm before I walked off. When I got to the corner of Frith Street and turned back I saw he had already disappeared into the crowd.

Acknowledgments

I wrote my first reported piece for the *London Review of Books* twenty-five years ago and I've been writing them ever since. That's almost half my life ago, and I'm still just as keen to leave the house and find stories. There's no gold medal for that, it's just a habit some people have, but it seems reasonable to believe that such work sets up conversations that novelists might not otherwise have, and that may not be a bad thing. In any event, the point about writing nonfiction is that you stack up a lot of debts doing it. I am particularly grateful, as usual, to Mary-Kay Wilmers, who started me off, and who encouraged these investigations into the human problems of virtual reality. I am fortunate in my publishers and editors—Jonathan Galassi and Alexander Star at Farrar, Straus and Giroux; Mitzi Angel, Lee Brackstone, and Eleanor Rees at Faber and Faber; Jared Bland and Kristin Cochrane at McClelland & Stewart—and I thank them for their work on this book. I am also grateful to my agent, Peter Straus. The book is dedicated to Jane Swan, who has helped me since the beginning, and I owe a debt of thanks also to Rachel Alexander, Jamie Byng, Sam Frears, Catherine Freeman, Deborah Friedell, Alex Garland, John Lanchester, Neil MacGregor, Jean McNicol, Lindsey Milligan, Edna O'Brien, Stephen Page, Allan Pederson, Martin Soames, Nicholas Spice, Harry Stopes, Josh Stupple, Inigo Thomas, Andrew Whitehurst, and Lynn Wright. In different ways these people have shown their friendship and pushed me on. If I went too far, or not far enough, it was because they stepped out of the room and left me by myself, which is where these stories begin and end.

—ANDREW O'HAGAN, LONDON, OCTOBER 2016

A Note About the Author

Andrew O'Hagan is one of Britain's leading contemporary writers. He has been nominated for the Man Booker Prize three times, and he was voted one of *Granta*'s Best of Young British Novelists in 2003. He has won the Los Angeles Times Book Prize and the E. M. Forster Award from the American Academy of Arts and Letters. He is the author of *Our Fathers*, *Be Near Me*, and *The Illuminations*, among other books. He lives in London.